Contents

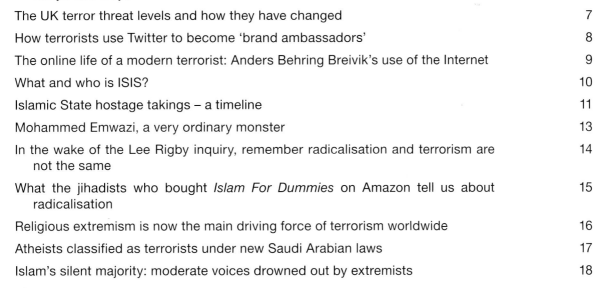

Introduction

Discussing Terrorism is Volume 283 in the **ISSUES** series. The aim of the series is to offer current, diverse information about important issues in our world, from a UK perspective.

ABOUT DISCUSSING TERRORISM

Terrorism is a chilling topic of conversation, but one that is all too relevant in today's society. This book examines both global and UK threat-levels, and explores issues such as the link between terrorism and religion, the rise of ISIS and the impact of terrorist activity. It also looks at the steps that are being taken to tackle terrorism.

OUR SOURCES

Titles in the **ISSUES** series are designed to function as educational resource books, providing a balanced overview of a specific subject.

The information in our books is comprised of facts, articles and opinions from many different sources, including:

⇨ Newspaper reports and opinion pieces

⇨ Website factsheets

⇨ Magazine and journal articles

⇨ Statistics and surveys

⇨ Government reports

⇨ Literature from special interest groups

A NOTE ON CRITICAL EVALUATION

Because the information reprinted here is from a number of different sources, readers should bear in mind the origin of the text and whether the source is likely to have a particular bias when presenting information (or when conducting their research). It is hoped that, as you read about the many aspects of the issues explored in this book, you will critically evaluate the information presented.

It is important that you decide whether you are being presented with facts or opinions. Does the writer give a biased or unbiased report? If an opinion is being expressed, do you agree with the writer? Is there potential bias to the 'facts' or statistics behind an article?

ASSIGNMENTS

In the back of this book, you will find a selection of assignments designed to help you engage with the articles you have been reading and to explore your own opinions. Some tasks will take longer than others and there is a mixture of design, writing and research-based activities that you can complete alone or in a group.

FURTHER RESEARCH

At the end of each article we have listed its source and a website that you can visit if you would like to conduct your own research. Please remember to critically evaluate any sources that you consult and consider whether the information you are viewing is accurate and unbiased.

Useful weblinks

www.asianimage.co.uk

www.churchtimes.co.uk

www.gov.uk

www.liberty-human-rights.org.uk

www.maplecroft.com

www.neurope.eu

www.newhumanist.org.uk

www.newstatesman.com

www.prospectmagazine.co.uk

safe.met.police.uk

www.timeshighereducation.co.uk

www.voxpol.eu

Terrorism and violent extremism

Get the facts.

What is terrorism and violent extremist activity?

Trying to define terrorism can be difficult and controversial, because so many people and countries see it differently. But any definition usually includes:

⇨ mass intimidation – trying to make lots of people scared to go about their everyday or normal life

⇨ unlawful violence or the threat of violence against the public

⇨ violence intended to change a law, culture or political system, or to change how people think or act.

Why does terrorism or violent extremism happen?

There are many reasons to explain why it may happen but whatever the excuse is, these are criminal acts that cannot be justified under any circumstances.

Who are terrorists or violent extremists?

They can come from any background, any community, or any religion or belief. They can be young or old, male or female, rich or poor. They believe that violence or terrorism is an acceptable way of changing how others think or behave.

Having extreme thoughts or beliefs is not a crime.

Using unlawful force or threats to support a belief or ideology is.

These criminal acts can include threatening someone because they are a different race, religion or sexual orientation; causing damage to property to get a political point of view across; or setting off a bomb to kill or injure people.

Why do people get involved in terrorism or violent extremism?

There are many reasons why this may happen. Here are just some:

⇨ a lack of identity or belonging

⇨ insecurity

⇨ defending their culture, way of life or beliefs

⇨ they may be pressured, or bullied into it

⇨ they may have been radicalised by violent extremist groups

⇨ they may want retaliation.

Those who encourage or get others to commit acts of violent extremism often target vulnerable people who are led into believing that violence or criminality can earn respect, riches or even glory.

However, even though a person may feel angry about something they believe is unfair this does not mean they should attack or threaten any person or any community.

Terrorism, violent extremism and the law

Any form of violence has a serious impact on victims and should not be tolerated, no matter where it takes place, or who's doing it. Terrorism and violent extremism is against the law, which means that anybody engaging in terrorist activity must be arrested and sent to court to be tried.

Terrorism can strike at the heart of any community and damage many, many lives.

What are the police doing to protect people from terrorism?

Public safety is of utmost importance and remains our priority, so we take terrorism and terrorist threats very seriously.

How we prevent and deal with acts of terrorism remains under constant review. This means we work closely with other organisations to protect the public such as central and local government, the emergency services and the British Security Service.

We constantly review how we police London, including where and when we send police officers to patrol the city.

We are trying to stop people from becoming or supporting violent extremists or terrorists in the first place.

We are working with many other organisations to help vulnerable people so that they are not led into a life of violence.

We are also addressing some of the reasons why people turn to violent extremism.

We are helping and supporting victims of 'hate crime' while making sure that people who commit crimes that are motivated by hatred of someone's race, religion or disability are arrested and put before the courts.

Terrorism can lead to some of the largest prison sentences that can be handed out in the UK, including life imprisonment. Between 2013 and 2014, 57 people were convicted of charges relating to terrorism and were jailed for 271 years in total.

⇨ The above information is reprinted with kind permission from the Metropolitan Police Service. Please visit safe.met.police.uk for further information.

© Metropolitan Police Service 2015

Recognising the terrorist threat

There is a serious and sustained threat from both international and Irish-related terrorism to the UK and UK interests overseas.

1. Threat levels

You can check the current threat levels:

⇨ in the terrorism and national emergencies area on GOV.UK

⇨ on the MI5 website.

The most significant terrorist threat comes from Al-Qaeda and associated networks. As the coordinated attacks on London in July 2005 showed, attacks may be mounted without warning.

Northern Ireland-related terrorism continues to pose a threat. Dissident republican terrorist groups (such as the Real IRA and the Continuity IRA) have rejected the 1998 Good Friday Agreement. They still aspire to mount attacks within the UK mainland and have conducted attacks within Northern Ireland.

2. Firearms threat

Although attacks involving firearms and weapons are still infrequent, it is important to prepare a plan. The essentials are to stay safe:

⇨ under immediate gun fire: take cover initially, but leave the area as soon as possible, if safe to do so

⇨ nearby gun fire: leave the area immediately, if it is safe to do so

⇨ leave your belongings behind

⇨ do not congregate at evacuation points.

If you cannot escape, you should consider locking yourself and others in a room or cupboard. Barricade the door, then stay away from it. If possible, choose a room where escape or further movement is possible. Silence any sources of noise, such as mobile phones.

2.1 Planning

When you are planning for a firearms or weapons incident, you need to consider:

⇨ how you would communicate with staff, visitors, neighbouring premises

⇨ what messages you would announce

⇨ how you would secure important parts of the building to hinder the movement of the gunmen.

You should integrate this firearms incident plan into your wider emergency planning and briefings. Test your plan annually. For further advice, liaise with your local Counter Terrorism Security Advisers (CTSA).

2.2 See, tell, act

If your organisation or an organisation in the area has been attacked, the more information you can pass to police the better.

See

Do not risk your own safety or that of others to get information. Use CCTV to check the area. You should think about:

⇨ the exact location of the incident

⇨ the number of gunmen

⇨ descriptions of the gunmen

⇨ the firearms they are using (for example, long-barrelled or handguns)

⇨ what they are carrying

⇨ their communication methods

⇨ the number of casualties

⇨ the number of people who are in the area.

Tell

Call the police immediately. Provide them with the information you have gathered. Use all channels of communication available to inform staff, visitors, or occupants of neighbouring premises of the danger.

Act

Secure your local area and other vulnerable areas. Ensure people stay out of public areas, such as corridors and foyers. Move away from the door and remain quiet until told otherwise by appropriate authorities, or if you need to move for safety reasons, such as fire.

Armed police

In an ongoing attack, the police may not be able to distinguish you from the gunmen. They may point guns at you. Follow their instructions and keep your hands in view. Avoid pointing, screaming or shouting, or any quick movement towards the police.

3. Vehicle-borne improvised explosive devices (VBIED)

VBIEDs can be highly destructive. Not only can the bomb blast be lethal, but flying debris, such as glass, can present a hazard.

VBIEDs can carry a large quantity of explosives to a target and cause a great deal of damage. The device can be delivered at a time of the terrorist's choosing, with reasonable precision (depending on defences). It can be detonated from a safe distance using a timer or remote control, or can be detonated on the spot by a suicide bomber.

The UK has a history of VBIED-based terrorist attacks which used fertiliser-based explosives dating back to the early 1970s. In 1998 in Omagh a device containing agricultural fertiliser (ammonium nitrates) was detonated, killing 29 people and injuring hundreds. In 1996 in Manchester, a device made from a mixture containing agricultural fertiliser devastated the city.

3.1 Planning

Vehicle access controls

Use robust physical barriers to keep all but authorised vehicles at a safe distance. You should ensure you have effective controls, particularly at goods entrances and service yards:

⇨ do not allow unchecked vehicles to park in underground car parks or service areas directly below public areas or where there is a risk of structural collapse

⇨ demand that details be provided in advance for any contract vehicles and the identity of the driver and passengers coming to your goods or service areas

⇨ deny access to any vehicle that arrives without prior notice.

Ask your local CTSA for advice on further measures, such as electronic surveillance (for example, automatic number plate recognition software) or options for protection from flying glass.

Physical security

Do what you can to make your premises blast resistant – paying particular attention to windows. You could have the structure checked by a qualified security or structural engineer.

You will need to balance the installation of physical barriers (for example, bollards) against safety requirements. Check your fire safety risk assessment and the planning regulations.

Personnel security

Organise and rehearse bomb threat and evacuation drills. In a VBIED incident, windowless corridors or basements may be safer than outside assembly points.

Train and rehearse staff in identifying suspect vehicles, and in receiving and acting upon bomb threats. Key information and telephone numbers should be prominently displayed and readily available.

The CPNI provides advice on hostile vehicle mitigation and NacTSO has published *Integrated security: a public realm guide for hostile vehicle mitigation*.

4. Suicide attacks

Suicide bombing is a very effective method of delivering an explosive device to a specific location. Suicide bombers may use a vehicle as a bomb or may carry or conceal explosives on themselves. The most likely targets are symbolic locations, key installations, VIPs or crowded places.

Explosions using homemade explosive devices have caused fatalities, injuries, and damage on a massive scale. The suicide bombers in the 2005 London attacks used precursor chemicals (in particular peroxide-based explosives) and killed 52 people and injured hundreds, many severely.

4.1 Planning

When planning protective measures for your site, you should consider:

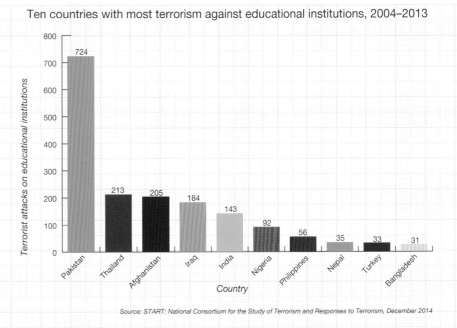

Ten countries with most terrorism against educational institutions, 2004–2013

Terrorist attacks on educational institutions

Country

Source: START: National Consortium for the Study of Terrorism and Responses to Terrorism, December 2014

- placing your vehicle access control point at a distance from the site

- briefing staff to look out for anyone behaving suspiciously or for suspicious-looking vehicles

- ensuring that all visitors have their identities checked

- installing a CCTV system.

5. Chemical, biological and radioactive CBR threats

There have only been a few examples of terrorists using CBR materials. The most notable were the 1995 sarin gas attack on the Tokyo subway and the 2001 anthrax letters in the United States. In 1996 in the US, an Al-Qaeda operative was sentenced for conspiracy to murder for his part in planning attacks using 'dirty bombs', which contained radioactive material.

The impact of a CBR attack would depend heavily on the success of the chosen method and the weather conditions at the time of the attack. The first indicators of a CBR attack may be the sudden appearance of powders, liquids or strange smells within the building, with or without an immediate effect on people.

Remember to apply personnel security standards to contractors, especially those with frequent access to your site.

6. Insider threat

Occasionally threats to companies and organisations come from within. Whether it is from a disaffected member of staff or an employee that has misrepresented themselves, there is more opportunity to disrupt or cause damage (whether physical or reputational) from the inside.

The risks posed by the insider threat can be lessened by carrying out thorough pre-employment checks and by having a strong security culture. The CPNI provides detailed guidance on personnel security.

7. Cyber threat

In the 21st century, one of the greatest threats to a company or organisation is from cyber attacks. The effects can often be devastating: the loss of crucial data, or a reduction in operating efficiency, or even closure.

Your senior management must assess the risk appetite of the company or organisation. But it is vital that everyone in your workplace understands the risks posed by cyber attacks.

A cyber attacker may not reveal themselves or even the nature of the attack. An attack may have no obvious adverse effects, but will extract information or data from your networks.

Read the advice on cyber security on the CPNI website.

26 November 2014

- The above information is reprinted with kind permission from the National Counter Terrorism Security Office. Please visit www.gov.uk for further information.

Number of suicide attacks by organisation from 2000 to 2013

The Taliban, Al-Qaeda and ISIL have claimed the most suicide attacks in the period. However, Hamas has proportionally used suicide attacks the most since 2000.

Organisation	Suicide attacks since 2000			Last Attack
	Total number of attacks	Number of suicide attacks	Percentage	
Hamas (Islamic Resistance Movement)	195	46	24%	2008
Al-Aqsa Martyrs Brigade	152	35	23%	2008
Al-Qaeda in Iraq	579	105	18%	2013
Islamic State of Iraq and the Levant	492	84	17%	2013
Al-Qaeda in the Arabian Peninsula (AQAP)	298	42	14%	2013
Tehrik-i-Taliban Pakistan (TTP)	778	97	12%	2013
Liberation Tigers of Tamil Eelam (LTTE)	499	35	7%	2009
Al-Shabaab	630	43	7%	2013
Boko Haram	750	37	5%	2013

Source: Global Terrorism Index 2014

Global terrorism fatalities up 30%, risk of attacks increase most in China, Egypt, Kenya and Libya

Over the last 12 months, global fatalities from acts of terrorism have risen 30% compared to the previous five-year average, according to a new security monitoring service from global risk analytics company Maplecroft, which also identifies China, Egypt, Kenya and Libya as seeing the most significant increases in the risk of terrorist attacks.

'The MTSD classifies 12 countries as "extreme risk," many of which are blighted by high levels of instability and weak governance'

The Maplecroft Terrorism and Security Dashboard (MTSD) is a new interactive mapping platform, which logs, analyses and plots all reported incidents of terrorism, piracy, political violence and human rights abuses by security forces down to 100m² worldwide. It also draws on Maplecroft's seven years of global data to reveal terrorism and security trends across 197 countries.

Globally, the MTSD recorded 18,668 fatalities in the 12 months prior to 1 July, up 29.3% from an annual average of 14,433 for the previous five years. Over the same period the MTSD recorded 9,471 attacks at an average of 26 a day, down from a five-year average of 10,468, revealing that terrorist methods have become increasingly deadly over the last year.

The MTSD classifies 12 countries as 'extreme risk', many of which are blighted by high levels of instability and weak governance. These include: Iraq (most at risk), Afghanistan (2nd), Pakistan (3rd), Somalia (4th), Yemen (6th), Syria (7th), Lebanon (9th) and Libya (10th). However, of particular concern for investors, the important growth economies of Nigeria (5th), the Philippines (8th), Colombia (11th) and Kenya (12th) also feature in the category.

Rising risks and economic costs in China, Egypt, Kenya and Libya

'Libya, Kenya and Egypt are among a handful of countries to witness a significant increase in risk in the MTSD and investor confidence in key sectors, including tourism and oil and gas, has been hurt,' states Jordan Perry, a Principal Political Risk Analyst at Maplecroft. 'When faced with rising security costs and decreasing safety for their personnel, companies can, and do, reconsider their country-level commitments.'

With terrorism incidents in Libya (10th) doubling in the last year, militia violence is having a toxic impact on the country's economy, especially its crucial oil sector which has all but ground to a halt following blockades of the country's main oil ports by rebel militias and divestment by multinational hydrocarbon companies. The flow of militants and weapons from Libya has also increased the risk of terrorism in Egypt (17th and 'high risk'). Attacks in the Sinai Peninsula and Cairo reduced tourist numbers by 20% in May compared to the same month last year, while frequent bombings of the gas pipeline in North Sinai have impacted exports and government revenues.

Tourism in Kenya (12th), which accounts for roughly 12.5% of GDP, has also been hard hit, due to the increasing frequency and intensity of terrorism attacks by Somali-based Islamic militant group Al Shabaab. June 2014 represented the bloodiest month since the Westgate shopping mall attack on 21 September 2013, with 69 fatalities and at least seven wounded. A single al Shabaab attack on Mpeketoni village, in Lamu County on 15 June was responsible for 48 of these deaths. Despite the deteriorating security situation, Kenya's strong showing at its US$2 billion debut Eurobond in June 2014 highlights continued investor interest in the country.

The MTSD also reveals that attacks are on the rise in China (32nd and 'medium risk'), many of which have targeted transportation hubs. Fatalities in 2014 have reached 76, compared to 16 over the first six months of 2013. The economic impacts of terrorism are so far negligible, but as China pushes for unconventional hydrocarbon development, foreign companies are likely to be involved in shale gas/oil exploration in the restive hydrocarbon-rich western

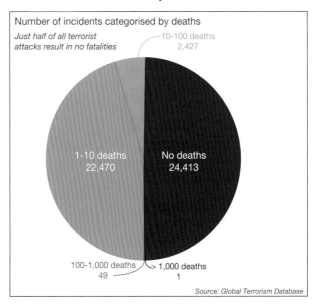

Number of incidents categorised by deaths

Just half of all terrorist attacks result in no fatalities

10-100 deaths 2,427

1-10 deaths 22,470

No deaths 24,413

100-1,000 deaths 49

1,000 deaths 1

Source: Global Terrorism Database

Xinjiang province, the frontline of Han-Uyghur tension. Increased repression in the region means the security situation is likely to worsen.

Terrorism in Nigeria is world's deadliest, Iraq endures most attacks

Iraq, rated as the highest risk country in the MTSD, recorded more than three times as many acts of terrorism as Pakistan (which had the second highest number of incidents) – with 3,158 acts of terrorism, resulting in 5,929 fatalities, an increase of 2,188 deaths on the previous year. The deteriorating security situation in Iraq underscores the Government's inability to combat the militant group Islamic State – formerly known as ISIS, which now controls vital oil and gas infrastructure, while threatening other key assets across northern Iraq.

'Iraq recorded more than three times as many acts of terrorism as Pakistan'

An intensifying campaign of violence by Islamic militant group Boko Haram has seen Nigeria (5th) record by far the highest number of fatalities per attack, reflecting the intensity of the violence there. The country has been host to 146 reported attacks in the period 1 July 2013 to 30 June 2014, resulting in 3,477 killed – an average of 24 people killed per attack, compared to two deaths per attack in Iraq. The increased capacity of Boko Haram – as illustrated by attacks on the key centres of Abuja and Lagos in June 2014 – is likely to lead to a further loss of investor confidence in Nigeria's ability to respond to security risks in the country.

'The dynamic nature of terrorism means individual events are impossible to predict' states Maplecroft CEO Alyson Warhurst. 'However, up-to-date global intelligence on the intensity, frequency, precise location and type of attacks can help organisations to make informed decisions relating to market entry, security measures for in-country operations, duty of care obligations, supply chain continuity and risk pricing.'

23 July 2014

⇨ The above information is reprinted with kind permission from Verisk Maplecroft. Please visit www.maplecroft.com for further information.

© Verisk Maplecroft 2015

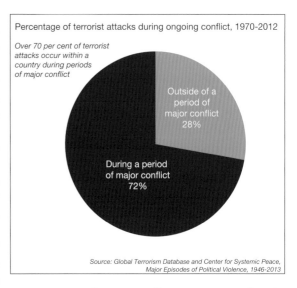

Percentage of terrorist attacks during ongoing conflict, 1970-2012

Over 70 per cent of terrorist attacks occur within a country during periods of major conflict

Outside of a period of major conflict 28%

During a period of major conflict 72%

Source: Global Terrorism Database and Center for Systemic Peace, Major Episodes of Political Violence, 1946-2013

Terrorism and Security Dashboard 2014

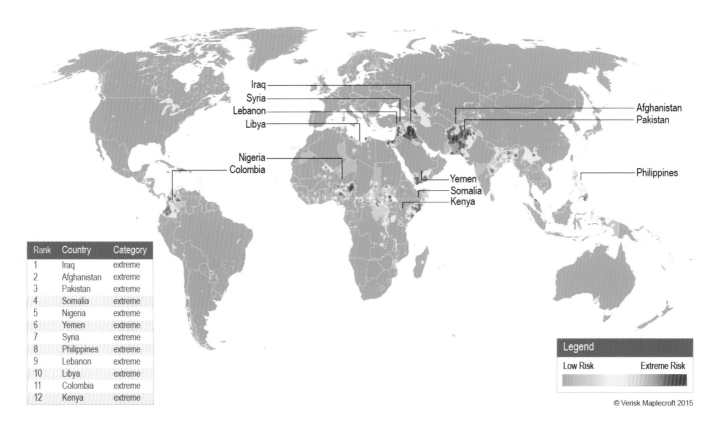

Rank	Country	Category
1	Iraq	extreme
2	Afghanistan	extreme
3	Pakistan	extreme
4	Somalia	extreme
5	Nigeria	extreme
6	Yemen	extreme
7	Syria	extreme
8	Philippines	extreme
9	Lebanon	extreme
10	Libya	extreme
11	Colombia	extreme
12	Kenya	extreme

Legend

Low Risk   Extreme Risk

© Verisk Maplecroft 2015

The UK terror threat levels and how they have changed

In the aftermath of the Charlie Hebdo shootings the UK's terror threat level remains 'severe', meaning an attack is 'highly likely'.

By Tom Whitehead

The UK terror threat level was only made public for the first time in the wake of the 7 July attacks in London in 2005.

There are five different terrorism threat levels which indicate the likelihood of a terrorist attack in the UK.

The different levels are:

⇨ Low – an attack is unlikely

⇨ Moderate – an attack is possible but not likely

⇨ Substantial – an attack is a strong possibility

⇨ Severe – an attack is highly likely

⇨ Critical – an attack is expected imminently.

Brought in by security chiefs in August 2006, the warning system was part of Britain's new counter-terrorism strategy.

It came a year after the 7 July bombings, in which 52 people were killed and more than 700 injured in coordinated bomb blasts on the Tube and a bus in London.

When they were first published on 1 August 2006 the threat stood at severe – the second highest level.

But just over a week later, on 10 August, the threat was raised to critical after police exposed a plot to manufacture and smuggle parts of explosives on to passenger jets flying between the UK and the US, and detonate them on board.

Counter terrorism police smashed the terror ring, arresting its members in a raid code-named Operation Overt, and on 13 August the threat level was lowered to severe, where it stayed for around a year.

Britain was plunged into a fresh state of heightened alert and the terror threat was raised to critical on 30 June 2007 after a blazing car loaded with propane canisters was driven into a crowded Glasgow Airport.

The attack came just one day after two bombs were discovered in cars in London's Park Lane and Piccadilly – among the capital's busiest tourist spots.

Police quickly arrested Muslim extremist Bilal Abdullah, a man behind the two attempted attacks. And on 4 July 2007 the threat level was lowered to severe, where it stood for two years before being lowered again on 20 July 2009 to substantial.

But the perils of terrorism came to the forefront again when on Christmas Day 2009 the now-notorious underwear bomber Umar Farouk Abdulmutallab tried to blow up a jumbo jet as it flew to Detroit in the US.

Tragedy was only averted when brave passengers overpowered the Nigerian, and terror chiefs decided to raise the British threat level on 22 January 2010 to severe.

It stood at severe for 18 months before being lowered on 11 July 2011 to substantial, where it stood for three years.

Home Secretary Teresa May announced the terror threat was again being raised to severe in August last year in the wake of warnings of the deadly threat posed by British jihadists radicalised fighting for Islamic State extremists in Syria and Iraq.

The level is set by the Joint Terrorism Analysis Centre and the Security Service, which operates out of MI5. It is independent of ministers and assesses a range of factors before deciding on the threat level.

8 January 2015

⇨ The above information is reprinted with kind permission from *The Telegraph*. Please visit www.telegraph.co.uk for further information.

How terrorists use Twitter to become 'brand ambassadors'

An article from The Conversation.

By Alfred Hermida, Associate Professor, Graduate School of Journalism at University of British Columbia

THE CONVERSATION

On an overcast afternoon in London in May 2013, an off-duty soldier named Lee Rigby was murdered near his barracks in Woolwich, southeast London. Rigby's killers were two young British men of Nigerian descent, Michael Adebolajo and Michael Adebowale. What people didn't know at the time is that six months earlier Adebowale had talked on Facebook about his desire to slaughter a soldier.

The authors of the official report into the killing chastised Facebook for not picking up on the threat, arguing there was a 'significant possibility' that the attack could have been prevented if the technology company had alerted the authorities. Politicians turned on social networks for not doing enough to stop extremists, accusing Facebook and the like of providing a safe haven for terrorists and of not living up to their social responsibility.

It's too easy to use social networks as scapegoats, especially when it distracts attention from the failings of the security services – who had previously had Adebolajo under surveillance. Extremists have always used whatever technology they could to get their message out, from printed propaganda to broadcasting over the airwaves. The smartphone is today's printing press, and social media a ready-made distribution network.

So it's hardly surprising that according to some estimates 90% of terrorist activity on the Internet takes place on social media sites. The real issue is about power: social media shifts the balance of power away from governments, police and the armed forces in favour of loosely organised groups of activists, dissidents, and extremists too.

Twitter guerrillas

Social media inherently favours guerrilla warfare, where a small, nimble force can successfully take on a larger, more unwieldy one. To understand how to combat extremism on the internet, we need to understand why this is.

Social media is generally free, open to anyone who can get online, and messages can be more visible than ever before, with a global reach. Instead of relying on the press or other intermediaries, extremist groups reach people directly and tailor the message accordingly. The Islamic State (IS) skillfully targets messages designed to spread terror among western audiences while recruiting followers with tweets aimed at the Muslim world.

Since social media operates as a network, it is much easier to spread hate from one person to another – each follower becomes a broadcaster – and the cost to reach 100, 1,000 or 10,000 people is essentially the same.

This distributed and decentralised model favours guerrilla tactics. Groups and individuals can operate independently, yet loosely connected. By contrast, messages from institutions tend to operate on a command and control structure, whose layers of bureaucracy make it hard to respond quickly.

Brand ambassador or terrorist?

It is much harder to shut down the propaganda channels of extremist groups when no one, and everyone, is in charge. Security comes through obscurity. Unofficial Twitter or Facebook accounts run by sympathisers are hard to track down as they can blend into the volume of stuff on social media. One study from earlier this year found 27,000 Twitter accounts that were positive about IS, yet none were officially run by the group. Instead, these people become what in the business world are called 'brand ambassadors'. In effect, extremists spreading hate are using the same tactics used by Hollywood studios to get fans buzzing about an upcoming film.

Twitter encourages us to live in the moment, to react rather than reflect. When news breaks, Twitter comes alive with a jumble of facts, speculation, rumour and emotion. The uncertainty that follows something like the Ottawa shooting provides fertile ground for an atmosphere of fear.

Tools of modern terrorist warfare:

#hate

twitter

The real-time nature of social media offers a tactical propaganda advantage to terror groups. They can try to seize the news agenda by sending immediate reports and photos from the scene of an attack, before the media or the authorities even have time to evaluate what has happened.

The public domain

The irony is how much of this activity happens in public, on networks that can be monitored by the security forces. As businesses have discovered, people are freely providing a wealth of information about their actions, intentions and beliefs on social media. Smart companies have learned to monitor in real time and respond rapidly to a consumer backlash on social media. There is a lesson here for the fight against terror.

Traditional, hierarchical institutions are slow-moving beasts that are ill equipped to fight in a propaganda battleground that favours the guerrilla tactics of the nimble.

The same qualities of social media that can help people to come together and protest about income inequality or contribute to the overthrow of a dictator can also be harnessed for evil. At the core of the debate is the fact that social media is a contested space, where the power of institutions and elites can be challenged and neutralised by those on the edges – for good or evil.

5 December 2014

⇨ The above information is reprinted with kind permission from The Conversation. Please visit www.theconversation.com for further information.

The online life of a modern terrorist: Anders Behring Breivik's use of the Internet

Did the Internet play a decisive role in Anders Behring Breivik's violent radicalisation? In a recent study of Breivik's online activities, I went through his posts on various message boards between 2002 and 2011, in addition to a collection of more than 7,000 of his private emails forwarded by Norwegian hackers to a Norwegian journalist six days after the terrorist attacks. I also attended Breivik's 2012 trial on a daily basis, which offered further insights into Breivik's Internet adventures and road to militancy.

My study led me to five main findings: first, Breivik never discussed his terrorist plans with anyone online. In fact, his online posts can hardly be described as extreme compared to some of the posts that appear regularly in the comments sections in mainstream news media. In other words, even if Norwegian Security Authorities had systematically monitored his online activity, it is unlikely that they would have responded.

Second, Breivik's critical views on Islam and socialism had been established long before the so-called counter jihad blogs were created. These blogs may therefore have played a less decisive role for Breivik's early radicalisation than assumed by many. Later on, however, the same blogs certainly echoed parts of Breivik's world view, although they come across as far less extreme than the ideological statements Breivik made in his own manifesto, in court, and from prison.

Third, Breivik's original intention was not to become a terrorist, but to become a professional author and publisher. He spent a lot of time and resources to establish a magazine for so-called cultural conservatives. It was only in 2009, when he was rejected by some of the people he admired and wanted to cooperate with – bloggers, politicians and online publishers – that he apparently decided to turn to mass violence, and started preparing the attacks.

Fourth, a prolonged withdrawal from family and friends as a result of extensive online gaming may have influenced Breivik's disposition to self-radicalise. In 2006, he moved back to his mother's apartment and took a year off to play computer games. Extensive online gaming continued to dominate Breivik's life in the years leading up to the attacks. Eventually, he stopped hanging out with his old friends despite continuous efforts on their part to include him.

This is not to say that it was the violent content of computer games per se that influenced his disposition for violence. Many people play violent games, yet very few engage in violence. Moreover, online gaming does not by definition lead to social isolation; it can be a rather social activity. In fact, the social dimension of online gaming makes it a potentially attractive alternative for someone experiencing difficulties in the 'real' world. The social commitments are smaller, and you get to be part of a team that, depending on the type of game you are playing, fights together against various enemies – some of them more adventurous and spectacular than others.

The potential danger of such an alternative reality is that it can be so attractive to some that they decide to spend most of their time in it, and gradually lose their connections to the 'real' world and the people closest to them. The latter are perhaps the only ones that could potentially prevent someone like Breivik, who already suffered from multiple personality disorders, from self-radicalising and gradually accepting mass violence as a legitimate means to an end.

Finally, the Internet offered Breivik the necessary knowledge and ingredients to build a large deadly fertiliser bomb. In fact, it appears that Breivik, through experimentation and dedication, was the first person to devise a bomb from diluted fertiliser. Measures to dilute the concentration of ammonium nitrate in fertiliser was introduced in Europe after the Oklahoma City bombing in 1995. The aim was to ensure that fertiliser products could never again be used to manufacture bombs. Breivik nonetheless managed to synthesize knowledge from hundreds of online bomb recipes to produce a very powerful bomb based on diluted fertiliser.

So, would Breivik have become a terrorist and a mass murderer if the Internet did not exist, all other things being equal (ceteris paribus)? No one will ever know for sure. There are several reasons to believe that the Internet intensified and boosted Breivik's violent radicalisation. It offered him a place where he could cultivate his radical views largely uncontested. It offered him relevant tactical skills and knowledge. And it offered him an alternative reality contributing to his gradual distancing from family and friends, which, in turn, may have been a precondition for his radicalisation.

On the other hand, the Internet is in many ways only a reflection of the 'real' world, and thus shares its unpredictable and complex features. It is what you make of it. While the Internet can be seen as a source for radicalisation, it can easily have the opposite effect too, depending on how you use it. We must therefore be extremely careful when drawing conclusions about the Internet's effects on particular outcomes. The Internet is perhaps more fruitfully seen as a means to an end rather than as cause to an outcome. As such, it certainly facilitated Breivik's violent radicalisation, but it does not explain it.

28 October 2014

⇨ The above information is reprinted with kind permission from VOX-Pol. Please visit www.voxpol.eu for further information.

What and who is ISIS?

The militant group offers a compelling proposition to would-be jihadists.

By Josh Lowe

What is ISIS?

It is a Sunni Muslim militant group operating in western Iraq and Syria. The name is an acronym, standing for 'the Islamic State of Iraq and al-Sham (the Levant)'. The group has dominated headlines this week after launching an assault on the northern part of Iraq, conquering the city of Mosul (population 1.8 million). With a reputation as ferocious fighters, they reportedly met with little resistance as professional security forces fled the city in the face of their advance. 'The city fell like a plane without an engine,' a local businessman told *The Guardian*. '[ISIS militants] were firing their weapons into the air, but no one was shooting at them.'

What does it want?

International recognition as an independent state for the territory it controls, which spans parts of eastern Syria and western Iraq. In this area, it functions as a *de facto* government, operating schools and courts. It also wants to control more territory. If it can sustain and consolidate its new gains in Iraq, it will control much of the northern part of the country, and reports say it plans to mount an assault on the capital, Baghdad (its advance has been halted just short of the city). It also wants to seize control of rebel-held areas in central Syria and potentially expand into the Lebanon to the west. In both Iraq and Syria, ISIS's enemies are Shia Muslims.

Who are its members?

Reports vary, putting the total number of recruits at anything from 3,000 – 10,000. According to Gareth Stansfield, professor of Middle East politics at the University of Exeter, the group tends to recruit most heavily among Syrian and Iraqi locals, but it does have some foreign fighters, mostly Chechens, Afghans and Pakistanis, as well as some Europeans. Michael Stephens, Deputy Director, Qatar, for the Royal United Services Institute (RUSI), says there could be as many as 300 Britons fighting for ISIS, and a further almost 300 other Europeans. The faction began as an Al-Qaeda group in Iraq, called the Islamic State of Iraq (ISI), but earlier this year al Qaeda leader Ayman al-Zawahiri publicly disavowed the group. Zawahiri reportedly considered the group too brutal even to be affiliated with his network.

How dangerous is it?

The group is well-resourced. Its new adventure in Iraq has seen it seize military bases in Mosul. In Syria, it controls oil fields, and it may yet gain control of Iraq's largest oil refinery in the town of Baiji. Stephens says that individual Saudi and Kuwaiti donors are giving money to ISIS, either through European financial institutions or, in some cases, by smuggling suitcases of bills across the border. It is also ruthless: the group has been blamed for a string of assassinations in Syria, including two alleged crucifixions. Most importantly, this particular militant operation is very good at recruiting people to its cause. 'This idea of fighting Shia seems to be really mobilising young men to fight in a way that fighting westerners didn't,' says Stephens. 'They [say] they're saving Islam from itself. There's something more nefarious about people from your own side turning against you.'

12 June 2014

⇨ Information from *Prospect* magazine. Please visit www. prospectmagazine.co.uk.

Islamic State hostage takings – a timeline

1 January 2013 — 1 January 2014

A timeline of Islamic State hostage taking

During 2013 a number of hostages were captured by the Islamic State group, or by others and then sold to IS. Amongst those kidnapped were British aid workers Alan Henning and David Haines and US journalists Steven Sotloff and James Foley – whose disappearances had not been reported under Foreign Office and US Government guidelines.

2 March 2014 — 30 March 2014

Three Spanish journalists freed

The Islamic State group freed three Spanish journalists during the course of March 2014 – Marc Marginedas at the start of the month and Javier Espinosa and Ricardo García Vilanova at the end of the month. Spain has denied media reports that it paid a ransom for their release.

19 April 2014

France reported to pay $18 million for journalists' release

Nicolas Henin, Edouard Elias, Didier François, Pierre Torres are released having been captured in June 2013. It was reported that the French Government paid $18 million for the four journalists' release. This has been denied by French President Francois Hollande, though he said negotiations had been ongoing for several weeks.

26 May 2014

Italian aid worker freed for $6 million

Frederico Motka, an Italian aid worker who was held alongside British aid worker David Haines (later executed by the Islamic State group), was reportedly released after the Italian Government paid a $6 million ransom. In January 2015 two other Italian aid workers, Greta Ramelli and Vanessa Marzullo, were also released from the custody of Al-Qaeda linked group Al Nusrah after the Italian Government paid a reported $12 million ransom.

19 June 2014

Family raises ransom to free Danish photojournalist

Danish photojournalist Daniel Rye Ottosen was released after a reported $4.3 million ransom, raised by his friends and family and transferred to the militant group by the Danish Government, was paid for his release. Mr Ottosen shared his cell with American journalist James Foley, who was executed two months after Mr Ottosen's release. On his release Mr Ottosen rang James Foley's mother to recite a letter he had memorised from Foley.

13 August 2014 – 19 August 2014

James Foley executed

James Foley is the first in a spate of beheadings videos released by the Islamic State group. Mr Foley had been captured in November 2012, at the same time as British journalist John Cantlie who remains in IS hands. A week before the video of his execution was released, Foley's family received a message saying he was going to be executed. The message did not include any demands. The video also included US journalist Steven Sotloff with the warning that he will be next if the US continues its campaign of airstrikes against the Islamic State group.

2 September 2014

Second US citizen beheaded

Two weeks later a video is released of the execution of Sotloff. It is thought that he was captured a year earlier near Aleppo, and was held in the Islamic State group stronghold of Raqqa.

13 September 2014

British aid worker executed

The first British hostage, aid worker David Haines, is seen executed in an Islamic State video. Mr Haines had been captured the year before in northern Syria and was sold to the Islamic State group. The video of his execution includes a threat to killed a second Briton, who is named the next day as another aid worker – Alan Henning.

20 September 2014

49 Turkish hostages freed

49 Turkish hostages are released by the Islamic State group – including the country's Consul-General, diplomats' children and special forces soldiers. Turkey said the hostages were released without a ransom being paid, without promises being made, and without a military operation. Many media reports expressed doubt over the Turkish Government's version of events – questioning why the Islamic State group would have freed the hostages.

21 September 2014 – 24 September 2014

IS affiliate kills French mountaineer

Jund al-Khalifah, an Islamic State affiliate, beheaded French citizen and mountaineering guide Herve Gourdel having captured him three days earlier. The group had threatened to kill Gourdel if France continued its involvement in a coalition of nations conducting airstrikes against the Islamic State group.

3 October 2014

British cab driver Alan Henning executed

Despite condemnation by Muslim leaders across the world over the impending fate of Henning, the Islamic State releases a video of his execution in October. Mr Henning, a 47-year-old taxi driver, was delivering aid to Syria and was captured half an hour after crossing the border into Syria at the end of 2013. He was affectionately known as 'Gadget' by the men who travelled to Syria with him.

16 November 2014

Islamic State militants execute US aid worker

A video is released showing the murder of US aid worker Peter Kassig – a former US army ranger who was captured in October 2013. The video also appeared to show a group of Syrian soldiers being killed.

January 20, 2015 – January 24, 2015

IS demands $200 million for Japanese hostages

In a video released in January the Islamic State said it would release Japanese hostages Kenji Goto and Haruna Yukawa in exchange for $200 million – the amount Japan had promised in non-military aid to help countries fighting the Islamic State group. Japan refused to pay the ransom and four days later IS released a picture of Goto holding a photo of the decapitated head of Yukawa. Goto had returned to Syria to try and rescue Yukawa.

27 January 2015 – 4 February 2015

Jordan and Japan negotiate for hostages

The Islamic State group said it would release Goto in exchange for Sajida al-Rishawi, a would-be suicide bomber held by Jordan. If the deal was not made, IS said, then a Jordanian pilot, Moaz al-Kasabeh, would be executed. The deal was not struck and Goto and al-Kasabeh were both killed – the latter was burned alive in a cage.

6 February 2015

Kayla Mueller killed 'in airstrike'

In response to the death of al-Kasabeh, Jordan executed two jihadists it was holding, including al-Rishawi. It also conducted 60 airstrikes against IS targets over three days. In those airstrikes, the Islamic State group said, another US aid worker, Kayla Mueller, was killed. The US Government has cast doubt on the IS version of events. Mueller, the last known US hostage held by the Islamic State group, was taken in August 2013 while leaving a hospital in the northern Syrian city of Aleppo.

⇨ The above information is reprinted with kind permission from Channel 4 News. Please visit www.channel4.com for further information.

Mohammed Emwazi, a very ordinary monster

By Suzanne Moore

I am not going to call Mohammed Emwazi by his cuddly nickname as the BBC headlines continue to do for some strange reason. I do not want to see any more pictures of him in his murder outfit brandishing a knife. I do not want to read any more details that seek to explain what turned him into a serial killer. He looks ill at ease in a Pittsburgh Pirates baseball cap. All the self-assurance of the feared executioner disappears when he is unmasked. Let's keep it that way.

Abu Ayman, an Islamic State defector, has said of Emwazi that 'Isis play him like a piano. He's a celebrity to attract our Muslim brothers in Europe. But some think he is showing off: they think he's being used by Isis.' Indeed. But none of this could happen if Isis weren't playing the global media like a piano. If we did not fixate both on his own image of himself in the murder videos or we didn't grab on to the smallest details of his life to try to make sense of his barbarity. It is a futile task and one that reminds me of how serial killers such as Ted Bundy or Peter Sutcliffe become notorious, while their victims remain nameless and forgotten. It is a bang on the head, a lonely childhood, some kind of dislocation, mother issues, father issues, a persecution complex, increasing paranoia. Such pathologies have always existed.

Now though there is a ready made ideology in which these traits can be exploited to make individuals feel special instead of ordinary, part of a bigger cause instead of being utterly alienated and now infamous for much longer than 15 minutes. The need to locate radicalisation in one place: a mosque, a school, a university is futile. We have enough evidence to show that there is no one route, nor is it the poorest or those without opportunity who are attracted to extremist ideology. They can be polite graduates, or high-achieving schoolgirls.

Yet ideological grooming operates much as sexual grooming does: the promise of the association with powerful people who will give you attention and make life's confusions vanish. Someone out there sees that you are very special; you will be taken care of. It offers escape from complexity. Severing heads from bodies will make you more famous than being a diligent IT worker.

So isn't our responsibility to stop adding to this 'fame'? To see Emwazi actually as a man who is not in charge but someone who has been used. To see him is to see that he is not actually even that interesting. His unmasking has involved the unmasking of Cage which was utterly necessary. Inevitably it has unmasked all kinds of fearful questions about the signs to look out for and how we stop such radicalisation. As the Internet seems such a determining factor in all of this, there is no simple answer here.

We could, though, stop contributing to Isis's own propaganda efforts and refuse to promote Emwazi as a celebrity jihadi or an icon of evil. Instead, we could ask what motivated some of his victims to become aid workers and journalists in one of the most dangerous places in the world. What kind of person does that? These are extraordinary people. Emwazi, on the other hand, is a very ordinary monster, an awkward young man wearing a baseball cap that is too big for his head.

2 March 2015

⇨ The above information is reprinted with kind permission from *The Guardian*. Please visit www.theguardian.com for further information.

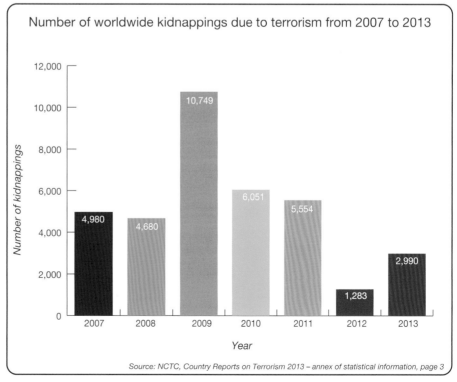

Number of worldwide kidnappings due to terrorism from 2007 to 2013

Source: NCTC, Country Reports on Terrorism 2013 – annex of statistical information, page 3

In the wake of the Lee Rigby inquiry, remember radicalisation and terrorism are not the same

An article from The Conversation.

THE CONVERSATION

By Matthew Francis, Senior Research Associate, Department of Politics, Philosophy and Religion at Lancaster University

A parliamentary inquiry has cleared MI5 of failing to prevent the murder of Fusilier Lee Rigby in May 2013. This despite the fact that his killers, Michael Adebolajo and Michael Adebowale, were both subjects of previous investigations by the security services – investigations which showed that both men had been radicalised.

Inevitably this conclusion has reignited the debate about how one can go about spotting a terrorist, and preventing an attack. If these two men held radical beliefs, why weren't they stopped before committing such a terrible crime?

But radicalisation and terrorism are often conflated. It is assumed that people who have been radicalised become terrorists, and vice versa that terrorists have radical beliefs.

This assumption is wrong, and indeed radicalisation is used to explain too much in many of these accounts.

Signs of radicalisation

The process of radicalisation tends to hinge on the beliefs of an individual. A person becomes radicalised when their beliefs have changed from being similar to the rest of society's – which are assumed to be normal – to beliefs that are quite extreme and possibly violent.

But how do we know what someone is thinking if they don't express their views out loud? When we ask about someone's beliefs, are they telling us what they think we want to know, how they like to think of themselves, or, in the case of violent beliefs, what they think will keep them safe?

One way to approach the problem is to look at what they talk about more generally. That includes their beliefs but also about who they are, what they fear and what they think of other people. This can provide an insight into their non-negotiable beliefs and values – what they hold to be sacred.

This approach might help us get an outline of someone's beliefs, and it might even tell us that these beliefs are very extreme, but it doesn't necessarily tell us how or whether they are going to act violently. As the Director-General of MI5 outlined in his evidence for the report, plenty of people express violent beliefs, the real difficulty lies in separating the doers from the talkers.

This is an important problem that is too often overlooked in the rhetoric about the threat posed by Islamic extremism. Plenty of people have extreme views but a liberal democracy doesn't set out to police beliefs and values. It should challenge violent beliefs but that is a very different proposition from criminalising them.

Terrorism, not radicalisation

Radicalisation is a different problem to terrorism so we need to be clear that we only criminalise people who express their beliefs and values in a way that threatens or hurts others, who incite people to act violently, and who express their intent to act violently themselves.

Adebowale's radical views, for example, became more specific threats in an online exchange with an unnamed person overseas that only came to light after Rigby's death. Adebowale stated that he wanted to murder a soldier.

This is crucial in this case. Had this information come to light earlier, MI5 would have made its investigation into Adebowale a top priority. What the security services can't do is prioritise an investigation unless the person under surveillance shows signs of planning an attack.

Talking about planned terrorist acts is not that unusual, even amongst self-starter terrorists. Research certainly suggests that in a majority of cases, lone-actor terrorists make their intent clear, possibly to family and friends and even in public.

The fact that Adebowale's communications about his plan were not shared with the security services will no doubt form part of the case to support the Government's attempts to increase powers for the security services. But we must be careful that this doesn't extend to criminalising people for expressing unpalatable views.

As we debate whether monitoring rules should be tightened, we need to keep in mind the fact that spotting that someone has been radicalised is not the same as spotting a terrorist.

26 November 2014

⇨ The above information is reprinted with kind permission from The Conversation. Please visit www.theconversation.com for further information.

What the jihadists who bought *Islam For Dummies* on Amazon tell us about radicalisation

By Mehdi Hasan

Can you guess which books the wannabe jihadists Yusuf Sarwar and Mohammed Ahmed ordered online from Amazon before they set out from Birmingham to fight in Syria last May? A copy of *Milestones* by the Egyptian Islamist Sayyid Qutb? No. How about *Messages to the World: the Statements of Osama Bin Laden?* Guess again. Wait, *The Anarchist Cookbook*, right? Wrong.

Sarwar and Ahmed, both of whom pleaded guilty to terrorism offences last month, purchased *Islam For Dummies* and *The Koran For Dummies*. You could not ask for better evidence to bolster the argument that the 1,400-year-old Islamic faith has little to do with the modern jihadist movement. The swivel-eyed young men who take sadistic pleasure in bombings and beheadings may try to justify their violence with recourse to religious rhetoric – think the killers of Lee Rigby screaming 'Allahu Akbar' at their trial; think of Islamic State beheading the photojournalist James Foley as part of its 'holy war' – but religious fervour isn't what motivates most of them.

In 2008, a classified briefing note on radicalisation, prepared by MI5's behavioural science unit, was leaked to *The Guardian*. It revealed that, 'far from being religious zealots, a large number of those involved in terrorism do not practise their faith regularly. Many lack religious literacy and could... be regarded as religious novices.' The analysts concluded that 'a well-established religious identity actually protects against violent radicalisation', the newspaper said.

For more evidence, read the books of the forensic psychiatrist and former CIA officer Marc Sageman; the political scientist Robert Pape; the international relations scholar Rik Coolsaet; the Islamism expert Olivier Roy; the anthropologist Scott Atran. They have all studied the lives and backgrounds of hundreds of gun-toting, bomb-throwing jihadists and they all agree that Islam isn't to blame for the behaviour of such men (and, yes, they usually are men).

Instead they point to other drivers of radicalisation: moral outrage, disaffection, peer pressure, the search for a new identity, for a sense of belonging and purpose. As Atran pointed out in testimony to the US Senate in March 2010: '... what inspires the most lethal terrorists in the world today is not so much the Quran or religious teachings as a thrilling cause and call to action that promises glory and esteem in the eyes of friends, and through friends, eternal respect and remembrance in the wider world'. He described wannabe jihadists as 'bored, underemployed, overqualified and underwhelmed' young men for whom 'jihad is an egalitarian, equal-opportunity employer... thrilling, glorious and cool'.

Or, as Chris Morris, the writer and director of the 2010 black comedy *Four Lions* – which satirised the ignorance, incompetence and sheer banality of British Muslim jihadists – once put it: 'Terrorism is about ideology, but it's also about berks.'

Berks, not martyrs. 'Pathetic figures', to quote the former MI6 chief Richard Dearlove, not holy warriors. If we want to tackle jihadism, we need to stop exaggerating the threat these young men pose and giving them the oxygen of publicity they crave, and start highlighting how so many of them lead decidedly un-Islamic lives.

When he lived in the Philippines in the 1990s, Khalid Sheikh Mohammed, described as 'the

principal architect' of the 11 September attacks by the 9/11 Commission, once flew a helicopter past a girlfriend's office building with a banner saying 'I love you'. His nephew Ramzi Yousef, sentenced to life in prison for his role in the 1993 World Trade Center bombing, also had a girlfriend and, like his uncle, was often spotted in Manila's red-light district. The FBI agent who hunted Yousef said that he 'hid behind a cloak of Islam'. Eyewitness accounts suggest the 9/11 hijackers were visiting bars and strip clubs in Florida and Las Vegas in the run-up to the attacks. The Spanish neighbours of Hamid Ahmidan, convicted for his role in the Madrid train bombings of 2004, remember him 'zooming by on a motorcycle with his long-haired girlfriend, a Spanish woman with a taste for revealing outfits', according to press reports.

Religion does, of course, play a role: in particular, a perverted and politicised form of Islam acts as an 'emotional vehicle' (to quote Atran), as a means of articulating anger and mobilising masses in the Muslim-majority world. But to pretend that the danger comes only from the devout could cost lives. Whatever the *Daily Mail* or Michael Gove might have you believe, long beards and flowing robes aren't indicators of radicalisation; ultra-conservative or reactionary views don't automatically lead to violent acts. Muslims aren't all Islamists, Islamists aren't all jihadists and jihadists aren't all devout. To claim otherwise isn't only factually inaccurate; it could be fatal.

Consider *Four Lions*. Omar is the nice, clean-shaven, thoroughly modern ringleader of a gang of wannabe suicide bombers; he reads Disney stories to his son, sings Toploader's 'Dancing in the Moonlight' with his mates and is pretty uninterested in Muslim beliefs or practices. Meanwhile, his brother Ahmed is a religious fundamentalist, a big-bearded Salafist who can't bear to make eye contact with women and thinks laughter is un-Islamic but who, crucially, has no time for violence or jihad. The police raid the home of peaceful Ahmed, rather than Omar, allowing Omar to escape and launch an attack on . . . a branch of Boots.

Back in the real world, as would-be jihadists buy books such as *Islam for Dummies*, ministers and security chiefs should venture online and order DVDs of *Four Lions*. They might learn a thing or two.

Mehdi Hasan is an NS contributing writer, and works for al-Jazeera English and the Huffington Post UK, where this column is crossposted.

21 August 2014

⇨ The above information is reprinted with kind permission from the *New Statesman*. Please visit www.newstatesman.com for further information.

Religious extremism is now the main driving force of terrorism worldwide

Previously, nationalist separatist groups were responsible for most attacks.

The *Global Terrorism Index* more or less does what it says on the tin – it assesses the number of terrorist attacks worldwide and the causes of those attacks. It draws on data from the US-based global terrorism database from 2000–13.

This year's report, by the Institute for Economics and Peace, recorded nearly 10,000 terrorist attacks and 18,000 deaths in 2013, a 60 per cent rise from the previous year. The increase was largely due to the ongoing civil war in Syria and the subsequent impact on Iraq.

The vast majority of attacks – 66 per cent – were perpetrated by just four groups: ISIS (Islamic State), Boko Haram, the Taliban and Al-Qaeda. All of these groups follow a Wahhabi ideology. More than 80 per cent of deaths from terrorism in 2013 occurred in just five countries – Iraq, Afghanistan, Pakistan, Nigeria and Syria.

This underlines a trend that the report's authors noted, which is that in recent years, religious extremism has become the main driver of terrorism. In years gone by, nationalist separatist terrorist groups, like the IRA or Chechen rebels, were responsible for the majority of attacks. Since 2000, the activity of these nationalist separatist groups has remained relatively stable while religious extremism – particularly in the five countries worst affected – has grown.

The report points out that religious ideology wasn't the only motivation for terrorism, and notes that many Muslim-majority countries – the UAE, Kuwait, Qatar – don't have a problem. It identifies three main factors that correlate with terrorism. These are hostility between different ethnic or religious groups; state-sponsored violence such as extrajudicial killings and other human rights abuses; and high levels of violence in general, such as conflict or violent crime. This demonstrates that 'social, political, and geopolitical' factors play a part, as well as religious ideology.

19 November 2014

⇨ The above information is reprinted with kind permission from *New Humanist*. Please visit www.newhumanist.org.uk for further information.

Atheists classified as terrorists under new Saudi Arabian laws

By Sara C. Nelson

Atheists are being defined as terrorists under a raft of new Saudi Arabian laws, a report from Human Rights Watch states.

The new laws are accompanied by a series of related royal decrees which appear to criminalise virtually all dissident thought or expression as terrorism.

'Saudi authorities have never tolerated criticism of their policies, but these recent laws and regulations turn almost any critical expression or independent association into crimes of terrorism,' said Joe Stork, deputy Middle East and North Africa director at HRW.

Regulations from the Interior Ministry cite 'terrorism' provisions to include: 'Calling for atheist thought in any form, or calling into question the fundamentals of the Islamic religion on which this country is based.'

Those who swear allegiance to any party, organisation, current of thought, group or individual inside or outside the kingdom are also included in the provisions. The Muslim Brotherhood and various Al-Qaeda factions are also among those on the list.

The new laws have largely been brought in to combat the growing number of citizens travelling to Syria to take part in the civil war, *The Independent* writes.

The legislation will address those who return with new-found training and ideas about overthrowing the monarchy.

Participation via forms of audio, written, visual media, social media, websites are all included in the definition.

Blogging for Al-Bab, Brian Whitaker writes that while the new laws might seem bizarre, 'in Saudi terms it does have a certain logic. Since the entire system of government is based on Wahhabi interpretations of Islam, non-believers are assumed to be enemies of the Saudi state.'

He also cites a 2012 WIN/Gallup International poll which found that almost a quarter of people interviewed in Saudi Arabia described themselves as 'not religious' and of those, five per cent declared themselves to be atheists.

Whitaker adds: 'Extrapolating that figure on a national scale suggests there are around 1.4million atheist terrorists living in Saudi Arabia.'

HRW describes the laws as having 'serious flaws, including vague and overly broad provisions that allow authorities to criminalise free expression, and the creation of excessive police powers without judicial oversight'.

While the law cites violence as an essential element only in reference to attacks carried out against Saudis outside the kingdom or aboard Saudi transportation carriers, crucially it states that inside its borders, 'terrorism' can be non-violent.

It can consist of 'any act' intended to, among other things, to 'insult the reputation of the state', 'harm public order', or 'shake the security of society' – none of which the law clearly defines.

Stork added: 'These regulations dash any hope that King Abdullah intends to open a space for peaceful dissent or independent groups.'

The HRW report concludes: 'Provisions of Saudi Arabia's new terrorism regulations that deny any ability to exercise basic rights of peaceful assembly, association and expression greatly exceed any notion of justifiable restrictions.'

2 April 2014

⇨ The above information is reprinted with kind permission from The Huffington Post UK. Please visit www.huffingtonpost.co.uk for further information.

IS THERE A GOD?

Islam's silent majority: moderate voices drowned out by extremists

An article from The Conversation.

By Ali Mamouri, PhD Candidate at the Institute for Social Justice at Australian Catholic University

THE CONVERSATION

Stretching from north Africa to east Asia, many Muslims are engaged in a life-and-death tussle with extremists who are bent on extinguishing the diversity of opinions within the Muslim community. Atrocities perpetrated by so-called Islamists grab the headlines: Boko Haram and slavery markets, the genocide of minorities and videotaped executions of westerners by Islamic State (IS) militants.

In addition to these atrocities, more mundane human rights violations are routinely carried out by theocratic regimes in Saudi Arabia and Iran. But what about the rest of the Islamic community? Why have their voices remained unheard?

There exists Islams, not Islam

Incorrect generalisations and minimisation of Muslims are offered up in explanation of every new terrorist atrocity. However, the reality is different from this perception: there exists more than one Islamic faith.

Islam is an umbrella term, which covers multiple differences within the religion. While Muslims hold similar beliefs concerning Allah, the prophet Muhammad, and the holy Quran, a wide diversity exists when it comes to the details and interpretation of religious doctrines. Tunisian Muslim scholar Abdul Majid al-Sharafi described this phenomenon as the 'municipality of Islam'.

Diversity of opinion is not a recent feature of Islam; evidence of broad shades of opinion can be traced back to its origins. But today the global Salafist movement, funded greatly by the Saudi regime and other sources, has great mosques, institutes, universities and schools. Its strong organisation and powerful media outlets enable them to publicly occupy most of the Muslim world and parts of Muslim communities in the west.

'Many Muslim scholars [...] believe that the Quran is not the words of Allah directly, but rather is the expression of Muhammad from his spiritual experience'

The Quran and terrorism

The Quran is typically cited as the ultimate source of terrorism and extremism among Muslims. This inaccuracy is based on cherry-picking selected verses; favourable words are accentuated while contradictory verses are ignored.

The reality is that the Quran – like the Bible and many other sacred books – uses religious language that is open to multiple interpretations. Many verses that could be seen as motivating violence can also be found in the Bible.

Muslims, like Jews and Christians, have a variety of interpretations of these texts. The word 'jihad', for example, is understood by Sufist Muslims as an esoteric term for fighting the evil instincts inside the human soul to gain ethical virtue.

'Incorrect generalisations and minimisation of Muslims are offered up in explanation of every new terrorist atrocity. However, the reality is different from this perception: there exists more than one Islamic faith'

Muslim scholars are also not in agreement on the authority of the holy text. Salafists claim that the apparent meaning of the Quran must be followed. Other schools of thought believe that this very simplistic view collides with the long historical distance between the revelation of the Quran and today, which makes the interpretation of the Quran difficult and requiring great expertise.

Many Muslim scholars, such as Nasr Hamid Abu Zaid, Muhammad Arkoun, Abdol Karim Soroush and Mujtahid Shabistari, believe that the Quran is not the words of Allah directly, but rather is the expression of Muhammad from his spiritual experience. For Muslims, this opinion opens the door for criticism of holy text and allows them to not obey parts of the Quran that are considered historical and not belonging to the core of Islam.

The same situation exists in dealing with Islamic history and tradition. For example, many Muslims do not consider the Islamic conquests that occurred after Muhammad as a religious action and criticise them strongly.

Is sharia law dangerous?

When people hear the term sharia law, what springs to mind are images of beheading, stoning, lashing and amputations in the name of Islam. While these do form a small part of sharia, again there exists a wide diversity of interpretations of sharia law among Muslims.

Sharia law includes the religious lifestyle of Muslims in both personal and social spheres. A significant part of it is acts of worship, personal status law and other regulations, including dietary restrictions concerning food and drink.

Sharia's most controversial element is the Islamic punishment law, which not all Muslims agree on. Some Muslim sects like Ismailism believe that sharia law is no longer valid. For them, sharia is just the ethical principles of Islam, which are mostly the same as other religions.

banned the political and juridical parts of sharia, and no-one has the authority to revive these laws today.

'Sharia law includes the religious lifestyle of Muslims in both personal and social spheres. A significant part of it is acts of worship, personal status law and other regulations, including dietary restrictions concerning food and drink'

Many other scholars, not just today but even in the first centuries of Islam, believe that wide sections of sharia are not essential parts of Islam and can be disregarded – just as happened with the Jewish Torah, which is not dissimilar to its Islamic equivalent. The traditional Shi'ite opinion is that their imams have

'Islam should not be considered from the perspective of fundamentalism as, in the end, this will strengthen the extremists' position'

What is agreed is that an overwhelming majority of the Muslim population has nothing to do with terrorism. However, they are under pressure from small but powerful extremist groups and religious regimes. The silent majority of Muslims therefore shouldn't be blamed for these people; they are instead victims of radical Islam themselves.

Islam should not be considered from the perspective of fundamentalism as, in the end, this will strengthen the extremists' position. Rather, it should be understood by opening a dialogue, supporting and co-operating with the moderates who offer a different understanding of Islam.

21 August 2014

⇨ The above information is reprinted with kind permission from The Conversation. Please visit www.theconversation.com for further information.

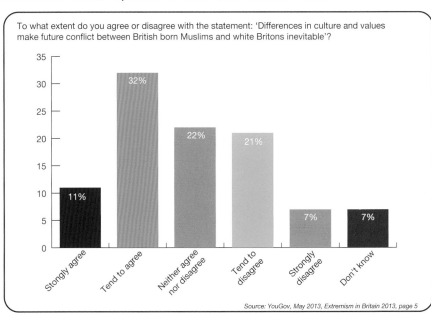

To what extent do you agree or disagree with the statement: 'Differences in culture and values make future conflict between British born Muslims and white Britons inevitable'?

- Stongly agree: 11%
- Tend to agree: 32%
- Neither agree nor disagree: 22%
- Tend to disagree: 21%
- Strongly disagree: 7%
- Don't know: 7%

Source: YouGov, May 2013, Extremism in Britain 2013, page 5

Protecting the UK against terrorism

Issue

The threat to the UK and our interests from international terrorism is severe. This means that a terrorist attack is highly likely.

The terrorist threats we face now are more diverse than before, dispersed across a wider geographical area, and often in countries without effective governance. We therefore face an unpredictable situation, with potentially more frequent, less sophisticated terrorist attacks.

The most significant terrorist threat to the UK and our interests overseas comes from the Al-Qaeda senior leadership based in the border areas of Afghanistan and Pakistan and their affiliates and supporters in other areas.

Actions

The Office for Security and Counter-Terrorism, in the Home Office, works to counter the threat from terrorism. Their work is covered in the Government's counter-terrorism strategy, CONTEST.

The strategy is based on four areas of work:

⇨ pursue: to stop terrorist attacks

⇨ prevent: to stop people becoming terrorists or supporting terrorism

⇨ protect: to strengthen our protection against a terrorist attack

⇨ prepare: to mitigate the impact of a terrorist attack.

We are developing and improving our work to protect the UK from terrorism. In particular, we are:

⇨ carrying out a communications capabilities development pro-

gramme, which will give us the ability to continue to protect the public in the future, as Internet-based communications become increasingly widespread

⇨ using science and technology to counter the threat from terrorism

⇨ supporting the UK security industry to export their products and expertise to other countries hosting major international events

⇨ working with the Northern Ireland Office and the relevant authorities in Northern Ireland to help counter the severe threat from terrorism in Northern Ireland.

Background

National Security Strategy

In October 2010, the Government published a new National Security Strategy which identified terrorism as one of the four highest risks we face. In the strategy we committed to giving top priority to countering the threat from terrorism at home and overseas.

CONTEST strategy

In July 2011, we published the third version of the UK's counter-terrorism strategy, CONTEST. The strategy set out the threat we face and our priorities for dealing with it through to 2015.

When we published the CONTEST strategy, we committed to producing an annual report setting out the progress we've achieved against the strategy's objectives.

Review of counter-terrorism powers

In January 2011 the Home Secretary published the findings from the review of the most sensitive CT and security powers. This led to three new pieces of legislation (see below).

Review of the Prevent strategy

In 2011 Lord Carlile of Berriew carried out a review into the Prevent strategy. After the consultation we updated the strategy. We now deal more proportionately with all kinds of terrorist threat and concentrate on some aspects of non-violent extremism that create an environment conducive to radicalisation.

Bills and legislation

Terrorism Act 2000

The Terrorism Act 2000 provides the legal basis for prosecuting terrorists and proscribing organisations (i.e. banning them from operating in the UK).

The Home Office publishes the criteria for proscribing organisations and a list of the organisations that are proscribed.

Protection of Freedoms Act 2012

The Protection of Freedoms Act 2012 repealed the stop-and-search powers known as 'Section 44' and replaced them with fairer and more specific powers.

The new stop-and-search powers enable the police to protect the public but also make sure that there are strong safeguards to prevent a return to the previous excessive use of stop and search without suspicion.

The Protection of Freedoms Act 2012 also reduced the maximum period that a terrorist suspect could be detained before they are charged or released from 28 to 14 days. Control orders were repealed and replaced with a more streamlined and less intrusive system.

The Act ended the use of the most intrusive Regulation of Investigatory Powers Act (RIPA) powers by local authorities to investigate low-level offences. It introduced a requirement that applications by local authorities to use any RIPA techniques must be approved by a magistrate.

Terrorism Prevention and Investigations Measures Act 2011

In December 2011 the Terrorism Prevention and Investigations Measures Act 2011 introduced the new system of terrorism prevention and investigation measures.

These measures protect the public from the small number of people who pose a real terrorist threat to our security but who cannot be prosecuted, or in the case of foreign nationals, deported.

Communications Data Bill

We published a draft Communications Data Bill on 14 June 2012. A Joint Committee of both Houses of Parliament scrutinised the draft Bill and reported on 11 December 2012.

The Intelligence and Security Committee has also conducted its own, independent, inquiry into the draft Bill, as this is an area that affects the work of the intelligence agencies. The Committee issued a summary of its report and conclusions and published its report, *Access to communications data by the intelligence and security agencies*, on 5 February 2013.

In their findings both Committees have recognised the need for new laws.

The Home Office has considered the Joint Committee's recommendations carefully and accepts the substance of them all. In light of this, we are re-drafting the Bill and the Home Office is engaging with interested parties on our revised proposals.

Justice and Security Bill

The Justice and Security Bill is being considered by Parliament. The Bill will:

⇨ make the Government and the intelligence services more accountable to the courts – it will introduce Closed Material Hearings in a very limited number of cases, so the court will be able to hear the case – and see all the evidence – regardless of how much information relating to national security is involved

⇨ stop people, including those with no connection to the UK, using the Norwich Pharmacal jurisdiction of the court to get access to intelligence material which, if made public, could compromise national security

⇨ make the intelligence services more accountable to Parliament for their actions – the Bill extends the Committee's remit and improves Parliamentary oversight so that Parliament, not the Prime Minister, will have the final say on the membership of the Intelligence and Security Committee

Who we've consulted

Over the last two years the Home Office has consulted with the public and relevant interested parties on a number of issues relating to counter terrorism.

In November 2010 we undertook a three month consultation process about the Prevent strategy – this resulted in a revised and updated strategy published in June 2011.

In March 2011 we consulted on a new code of practice for the use of closed circuit television (CCTV) systems and other similar surveillance systems.

In September 2011 we consulted on proposals to introduce a statutory authority to carry scheme, which would prevent individuals who pose a terrorist threat from flying to the UK. We published the Government response in April 2012, together with the final security and travel bans authority to carry scheme, which came into effect in July 2012.

In February 2012 we consulted on a draft code of practice for counter-terrorism stop-and-search powers](. This consultation followed the review of the counter-terrorism and security powers, which recommended that existing stop-and-search powers be replaced with more specific measures. Following the consultation we made a number of changes to the code of practice to ensure the powers are used fairly and effectively. The code of practice came into operation in July 2012.

In September 2012 we consulted on the operation of Schedule 7 of the Terrorism Act 2000 in order to ensure that the operation of its powers is necessary and proportionate. We are now reviewing possible improvements to the powers.

In December 2012 we consulted on a revised code of practice governing independent custody visiting for England and Wales. In March 2013 we published a summary of responses and the final code of practice.

3 September 2014

⇨ The above information is reprinted with kind permission from the Home Office, the Foreign & Commonwealth Office, the Cabinet Office, the Ministry of Justice, the Minister for Security and The Rt Hon Theresa May MP. Please visit www.gov.uk for further information.

Counter-Terrorism and Security Bill receives Royal Assent

Tough new powers to seize passports at the border from those suspected of travelling to Syria or Iraq will come into force within 24 hours, as the Counter-Terrorism and Security Bill today received Royal Assent.

The measure will bolster existing passport removal powers and allow police to temporarily disrupt individuals of concern who are attempting to leave the UK while further investigations are carried out. From today, the Home Secretary will also have the power to relocate those subject to Terrorism Prevention and Investigation Measures and require them to attend meetings with probation staff and others as part of their ongoing case management.

Other provisions – including a duty on specified bodies, including the police, prisons, local authorities, schools and universities, to have due regard to preventing people being drawn into terrorism; and measures which will enhance our border security for aviation, maritime and rail travel – are set to commence in the coming months, subject to Parliamentary approval of crucial secondary legislation before the end of March.

Clear evidence

Home Secretary Theresa May said:

The shocking attacks in Paris last month, in which 17 people lost their lives, and the many plots that the police and security and intelligence agencies continually work to disrupt, are clear evidence of the threat we face from terrorism. We have a fundamental duty as a government to ensure that the people who work to keep us safe have the powers they need to do so.

This important legislation will disrupt the ability of people to travel abroad to fight and then return, enhance our ability to monitor and control the actions of those who pose a threat, and combat the underlying ideology that feeds, supports and sanctions terrorism.

The events in Paris also highlighted important lessons for the UK – that whatever our nationality, faith or background, we must all work together as a nation to confront, challenge and defeat extremism and terrorism in all its forms, and stand up and speak out for our fundamental values.

The Act will also:

⇨ introduce new temporary exclusion orders, which will disrupt the return to the UK of a British citizen suspected of involvement in terrorist activity abroad;

⇨ improve the ability of law enforcement agencies to identify which device is responsible for sending a communication on the Internet or accessing an Internet communications service;

⇨ make Channel – the voluntary programme for people at risk of radicalisation – a legal requirement for public bodies so that it is delivered consistently across the country;

⇨ amend the Terrorism Act 2000 to put beyond doubt the legal basis of measures relating to the reimbursement of payments made to terrorist organisations; and

⇨ widen the remit of the Independent Reviewer of Terrorism Legislation and allow for the creation of a Privacy and Civil Liberties Board to support them.

Cross-party support

Use of the powers in the Act – which has undergone extensive Parliamentary and public scrutiny, and has received cross-party support – will be subject to stringent safeguards, including suitable legal thresholds and judicial oversight of certain measures such as temporary exclusion orders. And acknowledging concerns raised by universities and other education institutions, amendments made by the Government will ensure they balance their obligations under the new Prevent duty with the principles of freedom of speech and academic freedom.

During the passage of the Bill, the Prime Minister also announced an additional £130 million which will be made available over the next two years to strengthen counter-terrorism capabilities. This will include new funding to enhance our ability to monitor and disrupt terrorists and additional resources for programmes to prevent radicalisation.

12 February 2015

⇨ The above information is reprinted with kind permission from the Home Office and The Rt Hon Theresa May, MP. Please visit www.gov.uk for further information.

Britain's anti-terror laws are a 'complete mess'

By Katie Engelhart, VICE

At the tail end of last weekend, Londoners were given yet another reason not to want to go to work in the morning – the fear of being blown up on their morning commute. A hoax text message, purportedly from the Metropolitan police, was doing the rounds, claiming that 'every single police officer in the Met' had been called into work at 4AM to deal with 'a terror threat' on the tube. A lot of people saw the text for the bullshit that it was, but for those who did believe it, perhaps the hoax rang true because of the dread vibes emanating from Westminster recently.

The text came just two days after the UK raised its terror level from 'severe' to 'substantial.' On Monday, Prime Minister David Cameron announced plans to bulk up counter-terror measures in Britain. The plan would enable police to confiscate the passports of suspected terrorists. It would also, controversially, and maybe illegally, extend Terrorism Prevention and Investigation Measures (TPIMs), which allow for terror suspects to be relocated and for their mobile phone use & Internet access to be restricted.

Meanwhile, British officials continue their efforts to prevent British citizens from travelling to Syria. Scotland Yard claims that of the 500 British citizens who have reportedly gone to wage jihad in Syria, around 200 have returned to UK soil. In June, Cameron warned that terrorists in Syria and Iraq 'are also planning to attack us here at home.'

A growing number of experts claim that Britain's anti-terror measures strip innocent people of their rights and unfairly target Muslims. One such critic is Tayab Ali a London-based solicitor whose clients include the Muslim Brotherhood, in Egypt, and 'many, many' British citizens who have been charged with terrorism offences. Tayab, who regularly advises members of the British parliament on terror-related issues, agreed to have a chat with me. We talked about and the effectiveness of Britain's war on terror, and how it is felt by British Muslims.

VICE: On Monday, PM David Cameron announced that he would extend Terrorism Prevent and Investigation Measures (TPIMs). What is a TPIM and how does it work?

Tayab Ali: TPIMs are executive orders issued by the Home Secretary. They control the activities of individuals – in instances when intelligence suggests that those individuals could be involved in terrorism, but insufficient evidence to actually prosecute them.

What does that mean for a person issued with a TPIM?

TPIMs are onerous and control every aspect of a person's existence. They can be even more restrictive – and even more punishing – than an actual criminal sentence. TPIMs prevent a person from having regular and free contact with everyone else in society. They control who you can speak to, where you live and who

can come to your home. They restrict access to electronic devices including iPods, Play Stations and computers. TPIMs and their predecessor, Controls Orders, have been highly criticised, for obvious reasons. Controlees are not convicted of any offence in a court – and the intelligence used to initiate them is secret and cannot be directly challenged. In fact, an individual is not even made aware of why he is subject to a TPIM. One of my clients was placed on a control order and then a TPIM over a two-year period. He told me how he often considered suicide as an option to 'escape'.

TPIMs sound like a good idea on paper, but are not. They make communities feel like they are being persecuted. It would be much better to simply prosecute individuals when there is evidence to do so.

'The point is not that the laws are strong – it's that they are a complete mess, open to discretion and abuse.'

There's some debate as to whether Cameron's plan to let cops confiscate passports is legal. What's your view?

By removing an individual's passport or preventing British citizens returning to the UK, the Prime Minister is interfering with Britain's fundamental constitutional rights. The Prime Minister might do well to remember the fight against terror does not include rubbishing British values and riding rough-shot over our constitutional rights.

Wasn't PREVENT, Britain's counter-terrorism policy, meant to stop people being lured into extremism in the first place?

The government's strategy has failed in the most dangerous way. The Prime Minister's plan will not work because it does not address the root cause that inspires British citizens to join foreign military organisations, from the Islamic State to the Israeli Defence Force. It is inconsistent and smacks of bullying. But worst of all, it will exasperate the problem by further isolating members of our society. The strategy fails to recognise that people travelling to these foreign places are our people. They are not a sub-race of outsiders, programmed from birth to do us harm. We lost them along the way. Most of them were young children when the twin towers were attacked in 2001.

Our current threat level is the second highest it can be, with a terrorist attack in British mainland deemed likely. Any attack on British soil will be a direct result of the massive and repeated failure of the government's counter terrorism strategy and foreign policy over the last decade.

But isn't it fair to say that, over the last decade, we have seen a continuous strengthening of counter-terrorism legislation in Britain?

Britain was always slightly different to, say, the States – because we had the experience of the Irish troubles. Even prior to 2000, so prior to 9/11, there were pieces of legislation that were designed specifically to deal with domestic terrorism. In 2005, we had the London bombings. And a year later, you saw aspects of the terrorism legislation being strengthened. For example, supporting or glorifying acts of terror became substantive offences in their own right. But the point is not that the laws are strong – it's that they are a complete mess, open to discretion and abuse.

The Terrorism Act 2006 was meant to make it easier for law enforcement to arrest would-be terrorists at earlier points in an alleged terror plot, right?

What you're referring to is Section 5 of the 2006 Act, which concerns 'preparatory acts' of terrorism. The law is designed to catch people who the state thinks might become embroiled in terrorism later on. Section 5 can criminalise acts that, on their own, would be completely legal – if prosecutors can show that the end purpose of those acts might be terrorism. Often intention is proven using things like internet search history. I think this is very bad legislation. It is often described as 'thought crime'. And it doesn't apply in any other aspect of criminal law.

Can you give me a specific example of that happening?

One case I worked on involved a group of boys aged about 17 to 22. My client and his friends were in perpetual conflict with a group of other boys in their hometown. They met often and discussed how they might deal with the other group. They bragged and talked tough, but they never actually did anything. Separately to these conversations, the boys were involved in an Islamic group that regularly advocated its perceived Islamic grievances in public.

Eventually, the boys' conversations were picked up on covert surveillance. What they said in private was intermingled with 'mindset' evidence, ie. their Islamic advocacy, and my client was arrested and charged under section 5 of the Terrorism Act 2006.

Young Muslims run the risk of being criminalised for the very same things that non-Muslim kids do. If you have a bunch of non-Muslim kids playing paint ball or acting out James Bond fantasies, I doubt they would run the risk of prosecution. But the situation seems to change when you add the words 'Islamic' or 'Muslim' to it. I have even been consulted by worried Muslim parents, asking if it is lawful for their children to attend paint ball games, or whether that would be seen as terrorist training.

Have you been involved in any Section 5 cases concerning Syria?

Yes. The standard cases concern young Muslim men: people who have come of age in an environment where they feel rejected from mainstream society. Look, plenty of adolescent boys have a rebellious streak in them. But whereas a non-Muslim of that sort might go and join an anti-capitalist movement or Anonymous, some Muslim boys might get together with friends and discuss the crisis in Syria. While doing that, they might discuss the possibility of travelling to Syria to help out.

Have any of your clients actually gone to Syria?

Yes. The British government bears some responsibility for this. Its foreign policy has woefully failed to support non-violent democratic movements in the Middle East, leaving those who use violence to prevail. During the early part of the Syrian conflict, the British government championed the violent rebel movement that was fighting against Assad, as it did previously in Libya, against Gadhafi. This sent a strong signal to many that it was OK to go to Syria to join in – and that no criminal liability would follow. Clearly, this is not correct.

The British government's policy on these matters is incoherent and inconsistent. For example, I am often asked why British men fighting against Assad are prosecuted, while British men fighting with the Israeli Defence Force in Palestine are not prosecuted. The answer is political: it is the attorney general who decides.

As of his year, British citizens who travel to Syria are almost guaranteed to be stopped at the airport under Schedule 7 – and then interrogated and possibly charged with terrorism offences. Innocent people can find themselves at the wrong end of a prosecution.

To what extent is Section 5 used on Muslims, compared to non-Muslims?

It is completely disproportionate. Terrorism legislation is seen by many to unfairly target and silence Muslims. I have also represented people who have been accused of far-right extremism. In one particular case, I represented a white British chemist who was accused, under the Explosive Substances Act, of possessing potential bomb-making chemicals in suspicious circumstances. The case went to trial and the man was acquitted. Afterwards, when leaving court a juror approached the defence team and said, 'Do you know something? If he had been Muslim, we'd have convicted him.'

4 September 2014

⇨ The above information is reprinted with kind permission from VICE. Please visit www.vice.com for further information.

Anti-terrorism and human rights

By Nils Mulznteks

If you think that democracies can harmlessly forfeit human rights in the fight against terrorism, you should think twice. On 24 July, the European Court of Human Rights, the highest judicial body protecting the rights of individuals in 47 European countries, delivered two judgements which reaffirmed that absolute human rights norms, such as the prohibition of torture, must be upheld in all circumstances.

The European judges were asked to determine whether Poland had violated its human rights obligations in relation to the conditions of detention, interrogation and transfer to the US of two terrorist suspects currently held in Guantanamo, Abd Al Rahim Hussayn Muhammad Al Nashiri and Zayn Al-Abidin Muhammad Husayn, also known as Abu Zubaydah.

The seven judges unanimously found that Poland breached the European Convention on Human Rights on all these counts and on the failure to conduct effective investigations into the applicants' allegations. Indeed, the investigations only started a full three years after credible information emerged and they have been dragging on for five years, mainly because of undue political interference in the work of the prosecutors and the unwillingness of the US to co-operate with the investigations. Moreover, the judges condemned Poland's refusal to comply with the Court's requests for the submission of evidence and required the Polish authorities to obtain assurances from the US that Mr Al Nashiri will not be subjected to the death penalty.

This is not the first time that the Court exposes the lawlessness that has characterised the sordid rendition programme carried out by the CIA in Europe between 2002 and 2006, which involved abduction, detention and ill-treatment of suspected terrorists. Already in December 2012 the Court held 'the former Yugoslav Republic of Macedonia' responsible for the torture of Khalid El Masri performed by a CIA rendition team in the presence of Macedonian officials and for inhuman and degrading treatment during his arbitrary detention. It also found that the State had failed to comply with its obligation to carry out an effective investigation into the allegations of ill-treatment and arbitrary detention, as well as to provide an effective remedy to the complainant.

The significance of these judgements has a bearing well beyond the two countries directly concerned. At least 25 European countries have co-operated in the CIA rendition programme, but only very few of them have established some sort of accountability.

In the majority, little has been achieved. In Lithuania, in 2011, the Prosecutor General closed a year-long criminal inquiry, without pressing any charges. After international pressure and a national court decision, a pre-trial investigation was eventually re-opened last February.

The Romanian Parliament has conducted only a superficial inquiry. Both it and the Government have constantly denied the existence of any secret detention, in spite of evidence to the contrary.

In the UK, an official inquiry published last December raised several questions about the country's role in the US-led war on terror. Others, including Austria, Azerbaijan, Belgium, Bosnia and Herzegovina, Croatia, Cyprus, the Czech Republic, Georgia, Greece, Iceland, Ireland, Portugal, Spain, and Turkey still have to fully account for their co-operation.

If the El Masri, Al Nashiri and Abu Zubaydah judgements oblige 'the former Yugoslav Republic of Macedonia' and Poland to implement specific measures, they should also drive all governments to finally remove the cloak of secrecy they have drawn over their responsibilities. At the same time, these judgements provide two broader lessons for all democracies engaged in the fight against terrorism.

The first is that governments must not abuse the state secrets privilege to hamper judiciary and parliamentary initiatives established to determine responsibility for unlawful counter-terrorism acts. Though secrecy is sometimes necessary to protect the state, it should never serve as an excuse to conceal serious human rights violations.

The second lesson is that forfeiting human rights in the fight against terrorism is a grave mistake and an ineffective measure with far-reaching consequences, as it breeds contempt for the rule of law, a fundamental pillar of democracy and the values we stand for.

The US and European governments should make good use of these lessons. A first step would be to ensure that security agencies operate under independent scrutiny and judicial review. The next one should be to make anti-terror policies and actions more human-rights compliant.

By doing so, state security is not reduced. On the contrary, governments would increase their credibility among the public and weaken support for anti-democratic causes if they showed as much resolve in safeguarding human rights as in fighting terrorism.

31 July 2014

⇨ The above information is reprinted with kind permission from New Europe. Please visit www.neurope.eu for further information.

Countering terrorism

Human rights law requires the State to take steps to protect the right to life – which includes measures to prevent terrorism.

However, any measures taken to counter terrorism must be proportionate and not undermine our democratic values. In particular, laws designed to protect people from the threat of terrorism, and the enforcement of these laws, must be compatible with people's rights and freedoms.

Yet, all too often, the risk of terrorism has been used as the basis for eroding our human rights and civil liberties:

⇨ From 1969 to 2000 Parliament passed a number of temporary Prevention of Terrorism Acts, which included powers of internment and the removal of the right to trial by jury in Northern Ireland;

⇨ After the tragic events of 11 September 2001, emergency laws were passed which allowed for the indefinite detention of foreign nationals, who were suspected of being terrorists. Under this law, individuals could be detained for an unlimited period at a maximum security prison despite never being charged, let alone convicted, of any offence;

⇨ After a 2004 court ruling, that indefinite detention breached human rights law, detention was quickly replaced by the control order regime in 2005. Following the 2010 Home Office counter-terrorism review, control orders were scrapped in January 2012; but they were replaced with something almost identical, replicating the regime's worst aspects – Terrorism Prevention and Investigation Measures (TPIMs). Like control orders, TPIMs allow for indefinite house arrest, and other sweeping restrictions on individual freedoms, on the basis of largely secret intelligence and suspicion;

⇨ The maximum period of detention without charge for most criminal suspects is 24 to 96 hours. But, between 2006 and 2011, terrorism suspects could be detained for up to 28 days without charge. Despite this period being far longer than the period of pre-charge detention in any comparable democracy, Parliament also considered (and welcomingly, defeated) proposals first for 90 days, and then for 42 days, pre-charge detention;

⇨ Before it was repealed, section 44 of the Terrorism Act 2000 allowed people to be stopped and searched without suspicion. This overly broad power was used against peaceful protesters and disproportionately against ethnic minority groups;

⇨ Broad new speech offences impact on free speech rights, and non-violent groups have been outlawed;

⇨ Schedule 7 of the Terrorism Act 2000 is a breathtakingly broad and intrusive power to stop, search and hold individuals at ports, airports and international rail stations. It can be exercised without the need for any grounds of suspecting the person has any involvement in terrorism – or any other criminal activity. This means it can be used against anyone a police, immigration or customs officer chooses. Powers like this are ripe for overuse and abuse. They are invariably used in discriminatory fashion, with stops based on stereotype rather than genuine suspicion;

⇨ Most recently, the Government has passed the Counter-Terrorism and Security Act 2015, which again contains a raft of proposals as unsafe as they are unfair – including passport seizure and retention powers, ripe for discrimination; a regime of exclusion orders, which risks exposing British citizens to torture; statutory 'terrorism prevention' duties for a whole range of public bodies, including universities and schools; new data retention powers, mirroring those rejected as unlawful by the Court of Justice of the EU; and provisions which seek to breathe new life into the widely-discredited TPIMs regime.

We believe that terrorism can, and must, be fought within the rule of law and the human rights framework. Repression and injustice, and the criminalisation of non-violent speech and protest, make us less safe; not more. These measures act as a recruiting sergeant to the extremist fringe, and marginalise those whose support is vital effectively to fight the terrorist threat.

They also undermine the values that separate us from the terrorist – the very values we should be fighting to protect.

Overview of terrorism legislation

There are numerous Acts of Parliament and regulations, rules and Orders which provide for special counter-terrorism powers and offences.

And all of this is in addition to ordinary criminal offences, and police and security services' powers of surveillance and investigation.

While some of these new laws and specific terrorism offences may be necessary, many others are not. Much recent counter-terrorism legislation is dangerously over-broad and has affected vast numbers of people, in particular peaceful protesters and ethnic minority groups, thereby undermining civil liberties and fundamental human rights.

The worst excesses of counter-terror law passed since 2000 include:

⇨ Indefinite detention without charge of foreign nationals if suspected of involvement in terrorism;

- Unsafe and unfair control orders imposing severe and intrusive prohibitions, including indefinite house arrest for up to 16 hours a day without charge, let alone conviction;

- Pre-charge detention in terrorism cases, currently allowing for 14-day detention without charge - the longest period of any comparable democracy;

- Section 44 of the Terrorism Act 2000, allowing stop and search without suspicion (thankfully now repealed), which was disproportionately used against peaceful protesters and ethnic minority groups.

Other counter-terrorism laws that raise grave concerns include:

- The dangerously broad definition of 'terrorism', which applies to action taken to advance any 'political, religious, racial or ideological' cause designed to influence the government of any country or international organisation or to intimidate any member of the public anywhere in the world. Many offences are linked to this definition of terrorism, which means that large numbers are potentially criminalised. The definition stretches to action which is designed to seriously disrupt an electronic system;

- Broad new speech offences, including the 'encouragement of terrorism' which encompasses making statements that glorify terrorist acts. It is an offence even if the person or group making the statement doesn't intend to encourage terrorism. As the definition of terrorism is so wide, this could criminalise people speaking out against repressive regimes anywhere in the world. These offences have the potential to seriously infringe free speech rights, criminalising careless talk and having a chilling effect on free speech surrounding, for example, foreign policy;

- the offence of photographing anything that might be useful to someone committing or preparing an act of terrorism. This measure has seen many tourists and professional photographers stopped from taking photos of police officers or landmark buildings;

- The banning of non-violent political organisations, amounting effectively to state censorship of political views, which has the potential to drive debate underground;

- The power given to a constable, immigration officer or customs officer at a port or border to question, detain and (for the police) to take the DNA of anyone entering or leaving the UK to determine whether they are involved in some way in acts of terrorism – a power that can be exercised without any reasonable suspicion of such involvement;

- The extraordinarily broad powers under the Civil Contingencies Act 2004, which allow a Minister, whenever there is the threat of terrorism, to make emergency regulations that could temporarily override almost all other legislation.

- The latest raft of unsafe and unfair proposals contained in the Government's Counter-Terrorism and Security Act 2015, which include passport seizure and retention powers; exclusion orders; and yet more data retention measures.

In July 2010, the Coalition Government bound itself together with the language of civil liberties. It promptly announced a wide-ranging review into counter-terrorism measures. Many of these proposals were then brought into effect by the Protection of Freedoms Act 2012.

With this latest terrorism legislation, however, the very same Government abrogates its fledgling commitment to ensure that we do not abandon our values in the fight against terror. In confronting an ugly ideology that promotes arbitrary violence, the subjugation of women and tyranny, we would expect political leaders to promote, robustly and actively, democratic values such as the rule of law, human rights and equal treatment. Instead, the Counter-Terrorism and Security Act 2015 plays into the hands of terrorists, by allowing them to shape our laws in a way that undermines our principles.

Updated April 2015

- The above information is reprinted with kind permission from Liberty. Please visit www.liberty-human-rights.org.uk for further information.

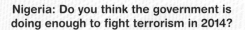

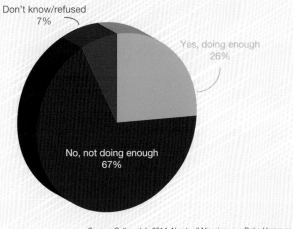

Source: Gallup, July 2014, Nearly all Nigerians see Boko Haram as a Major Threat

What about the Britons who fight for Israel?

By Patrick Worrall

The claim

'We have British citizens going over to fight in the Israeli army. Yesterday we know they are taking part in the collective punishment of a civilian population. That's a crime.'

Farooq Siddiqui, 3 July 2014

An ex-adviser to the Government on tackling extremism in Britain's Muslim communities raised an interesting point on Channel 4 News in relation to Brits who fight in conflicts abroad.

Farooq Siddiqui, formerly of the Prevent programme, is calling for the UK to stop criminalising young Muslims who travel to Syria to fight against Bashar al-Assad.

Security service estimates suggest around 500 Britons have travelled to Syria to take part in the civil war.

Mr Siddiqui asked why the Government has threatened to arrest British Muslims who return from Syria while it allows young people to fight for Israel and other countries with impunity.

'If we're talking about stopping people, Muslims, stopping them from going over to other countries and fighting, why are we not doing that as a blanket for stopping anyone that goes over abroad to fight in other countries?'

Is Mr Siddiqui right to say that young Brits are fighting for the Israel Defense Forces (IDF) while the Israelis are engaged in controversial strikes against Palestinian targets following the murder of three Jewish teenagers?

The analysis

Most Israeli citizens are obliged to do national service of up to two-and-a-half years in the country's military, and so a significant number of British-born Israelis or immigrants with dual nationality will inevitably join Israel's armed forces for a spell.

But you don't have to be a citizen of the Jewish state to fight for the IDF.

The Israeli military runs a programme called 'mahal' which allows non-Israeli nationals of Jewish descent to join the ranks of the armed forces for an 18-month tour of duty.

According to the rules, British men under 24 or women under 21 who have one parent or grandparent who is or was Jewish are eligible.

That's Jewish (you need to prove it by getting a rabbi to sign a confirmation) not Israeli.

Overseas recruits get the same pay and conditions as Israelis and 'serve always shoulder to shoulder with regular Israeli soldiers'.

The numbers of volunteers from the UK are small but significant: the IDF told Channel 4 News there are 'around one hundred Brits currently serving' in its ranks.

There is a even a support group for British parents of IDF soldiers called Mahal Mums.

We're not aware of anyone questioning the legality of this arrangement.

Unlike some other countries, Britain does not have an effective law prohibiting its citizens from fighting for foreign armies.

There is an obscure piece of legislation still on the statute books – the Foreign Enlistment Act 1870 – which ostensibly makes it illegal for British citizens to join the armed forces of a country fighting a state at peace with Britain.

But this proved to be embarrassingly ineffective when prosecutors attempted to stop British volunteers from fighting in the Spanish Civil War in the 1930s.

The lack of any practical ban on foreign enlistment leads to the slightly odd situation where a teenager can travel to Syria to fight for the brutal Assad regime with impunity, but if he

sides with enemies of the regime he could face prosecution as a terrorist back in Britain.

This is because of the broad scope of anti-terror legislation. In the Queen's Speech last month, the government set out new laws which mean Brits who travel overseas to train for acts of terrorism against any government will be prosecuted as if their actions had taken place in the UK.

In May Mashudur Choudhury, 31, from Portsmouth, became the first Briton to be convicted of engaging in conduct in preparation for terrorist acts after attending a training camp in Syria.

Choudhury wasn't threatening the UK, he was training to fight Assad – who David Cameron also wanted to target with military action before losing a Commons vote last year.

But a supreme court judgement from last year ruled that the legal definition of terrorism can include 'any or all military attacks by a non-state armed group against any or all state or inter-governmental organisation armed forces in the context of a non-international armed conflict'.

So if someone fights in a civil war against a regime the British Government hates – even if they fight for a moderate faction not banned as a terror organisation – they can still be prosecuted as a terrorist.

War crimes?

Mr Siddiqui is not the only person to have accused Israel of war crimes over its recent actions in the West Bank and Gaza in the wake of the killings of three Israeli teens.

Amnesty International has echoed his use of the words 'collective punishment', saying: 'Justice will not be served by Israel seeking revenge by imposing collective punishment, or committing other violations of Palestinians' rights.'

Collective punishment against a civilian population is banned under the fourth Geneva Convention.

But in the absence of any legal case brought against the IDF, the suggestion that Israeli air strikes, arrests, shootings and demolition of buildings constitute 'collective punishment' of the Palestinians remains an unproven allegation.

How likely is it that Britons have been directly involved in clashes with Palestinians in recent days? Not surprisingly, we don't have information on the movements of individual IDF soldiers.

But there is no reason why they would not be involved. The rules of mahal state that overseas recruits are liable to be picked for the same frontline combat units as Israeli conscripts, including infantry, tanks and special forces.

The verdict

It was news to FactCheck, but there are around 100 British nationals serving with the IDF as we speak, apparently with no legal difficulties.

But a Brit who trains or fights with any anti-Assad rebel group runs the risk of being jailed as a terrorist.

If we are worried about young British Muslims heading off to the Middle East to receive military training, should we be equally worried about Jews?

That depends on whether Mr Siddiqui is justified in comparing the experience of serving in a professional army overseas to fighting alongside Islamist militant groups in Syria. Of course this is a politically-charged and highly debatable point.

He insisted in the interview: 'It is a fighting force, whether you want to say it's disciplined or it's a militia. The effect on the individual, the effect on the combatant is still the same.'

7 July 2014

⇨ The above information is reprinted with kind permission from Channel 4 News. Please visit www.channel4.com for further information.

Universities must not become part of the security apparatus

The Counter-Terrorism Bill will co-opt academics into the 'securocrat' and chill debate on campus – it must be fought, says Martin Hall.

Imagine this. You're teaching a course on current affairs and decide to have your class debate the merits and demerits of fracking. The debate is passionate and gets out of hand, with students on both sides getting personal. You calm them down, and the session ends. But you've noticed that one student, a passionate environmentalist, is sullen and withdrawn, not engaging with others, and obviously anxious. You are under a standing instruction from your dean to report all such symptoms to the faculty administrator. Next week, the student is absent. You learn that, based on your report, she is now under the supervision of your university's local authority, with a support plan to help correct her radical tendencies.

Now consider this. The Counter-Terrorism and Security Bill 2014–15 being considered by Parliament proposes that all university governing bodies have a statutory duty to implement measures that prevent radicalisation that could lead to acts of terrorism. In addition to barring radical advocates from speaking on campuses, the new law will require every local authority to set up a panel to which the police can refer 'identified individuals' who are considered to be vulnerable to radicalisation. All universities are identified as 'partners' with their local authorities in this process of referral.

The Government's focus is, of course, on the acute threat posed by the conflicts in Syria, Iraq, Pakistan and Afghanistan. But one of the objectives of extreme and unpredictable violence is to create a syndrome of responses that, in themselves, promote ever more violent reactions. Will this new act achieve its immediate aim of preventing Islamic radicalisation?

Or will these new statutory duties of referral push those who are singled out down a path that they may otherwise have rejected? The new law is not directed at Muslims alone, but at anyone with radical views, including views that are non-violent but that might open up a road to violence. Could these new statutory obligations on universities be used against opponents of fracking, or animal rights activists, or anti-nuclear movements, or any radical opposition to the status quo? And where would that leave the principles of academic freedom and freedom of speech in universities, and elsewhere?

Here is Baroness Kennedy of The Shaws' summation of one of the key issues, in her questioning of James Brokenshire, the Minister for Security and Immigration, on 3 December: 'The nature of the university is to develop the mind. It is about the whole business of freedom of speech. Freedom of exchange of ideas is at the heart of the university. By challenging orthodoxies, people grow in ideas. Inevitably, some of those ideas will be bad ones, but the best way to deal with them is in debate and by challenging them in the process of learning. No university has created a fundamentalist who has gone to Syria to take part in what is going on there. Yes, people may have been influenced, probably more by other students. That can happen in a cafe in Birmingham as much as in any university. You are introducing a chilling effect on the whole thing that universities are about, which you and I benefited from, as did most people who went to university – and 40 per cent of our young now go to university. You are doing this when we know that universities up and down the land are already considering these issues and thinking about how they might deal with them and how they might create the debate, without having a statutory duty to do so. That is what concerns people: the statutory duty with a power to give directions from the state. The state will be able to tell universities what they ought to do, and they will be punished in some way if they do not fulfil the requirement set by the state and government... I want you to explain to us why it needs to be a statutory duty.'

Universities, then, already work extensively with the police in the context of the existing Home Office policy for countering radicalisation, known as 'Prevent'. The new law will make Prevent a statutory responsibility rather than a voluntary programme.

But there is a significant counter argument: that Prevent, in itself, angers and radicalises students. This is because of the implication that, simply by virtue of holding Islamic beliefs, a person is more likely to become a terrorist. The same assumption is not made about, say, Catholics. Given that the 2011 Census recorded 2.7 million Muslims living in the UK and that the Home Office is currently concerned about 500 individuals, there is a question of effectiveness and proportionality for the Prevent strategy as it is, let alone for the draconian expansion of powers contemplated for the new act.

The draft legislation also proposes processes of referral for students considered at risk of succumbing to radicalisation. Universities will be required to train all staff who have contact with students to recognise what Brokenshire called being 'withdrawn and reserved, and perhaps showing other personality traits'. Where these traits are identified, the university must refer the student to a panel set up by the police and the local authority. This panel will oversee and administer a safeguarding programme, which may include referral to the health services.

This aspect of the Bill has alarmed Sir Peter Fahy, chief constable of the Greater Manchester Police and the national lead for Prevent. 'If these issues [defining extremism] are left to securocrats then there is a danger of a drift to a police state,' he told a national newspaper last month. 'I am a securocrat; it's people like me, in the security services, people with a narrow responsibility for counter -terrorism. It is better for that to be defined by wider society and not securocrats. There is a danger of us being turned into a thought police. This securocrat says we do not want to be in the space of policing thought or police defining what is extremism.'

Both the Bill and the current government consultation make it clear that these measures will also apply to

'non-violent extremism, which can create an atmosphere conducive to terrorism and can popularise views which terrorists exploit'. This means that the statutory responsibilities to be introduced in the Act could be used by the police and local authorities in circumstances such as those recently faced by Canterbury Christ Church University, which was asked for a list of those attending a debate about and discussion of fracking.

What would happen if a university, or an individual staff member, declined to take part in Prevent or refused to refer students showing specified personality traits to local authority panels? Kennedy pushed Brokenshire repeatedly on this and eventually got her answer: a charge of contempt of court and, perhaps, prison.

The Bill was due to have its third reading in Parliament this week and is open for public consultation until 30 January. It raises issues that must be taken seriously.

8 January 2015

⇨ The above information is reprinted with kind permission from Times Higher Educaiton. Please visit www.timeshighereducation.co.uk for further information.

Anti-radicalisation policies proposed for school classes

By Margaret Holness, Education Correspondent

Front-line schools, including church schools in ethnically mixed urban conurbations, are likely to be those most affected by the Counter-Terrorism and Security Bill, introduced into Parliament on Wednesday.

The Bill will place a statutory duty on schools, colleges, and universities to put in place anti-radicalisation policies and ban visits from extremist speakers. Similar provisions will apply to prisons and local councils. The Bill has all-party support, and is likely to become law by Christmas.

Commenting on the implications of the Bill for schools, the Church of England's chief education officer, the Revd Nigel Genders, said: 'We need to take the threat of terrorism very seriously, and we are committed to being part of the solution.

'But if schools are to be held to account, they need very clear advice about how they can prevent young people being drawn into terrorism. We don't want just to prevent the development of extremist views, but to promote a positive vision. This includes effective religious

education that teaches pupils that those who advocate violence, hatred, and intolerance are distorting their particular faith.'

This week, teachers' leaders accepted that schools had a part to play. The general secretary of the Association of School and College Leaders, Brian Lightman, said that the task for schools and colleges was to divert young people from organisations that held unacceptable extremist views. 'We are preparing guidance for school and college leaders, setting out actions they can and should take when they suspect young people may be vulnerable to radicalisation or extremism.'

But he warned members 'to be careful about making assumptions... It is not necessarily the case that, because a vulnerable young person behaves in a certain way, or has certain experiences, he or she is either committed to extremist ideology or may become a terrorist.'

The general secretary of the National Association of Head Teachers, Russell Hobby, said that schools had a duty to protect children and neighbourhoods. But he also said: 'They are not a police service. A school's main contribution to the cause of anti-extremism is to provide a balanced curriculum and a safe environment where human rights are respected.' Where school leaders saw signs that students were at risk of radicalisation, they should involve specialist agencies, he said.

Intensive lessons on the dangers of Islamic extremism were already taking place at Sir John Cass and Redcoat School, in east London, last week as the Church of England school – one of the most successful of its kind in the country – was placed in special measures by OFSTED, writes Margaret Holness.

The reason given by inspectors was: 'The school has not put in place steps to ensure that students, staff and governors understand the risks posed by extremism.'

The 1,500-pupil comprehensive, where more than 90 per cent of pupils are of Bangladeshi heritage, lost its previous 'outstanding' status after a snap inspection by OFSTED in September, which confirmed suspicions that some members of the sixth-form Islamic Society were misusing social media, including a dedicated school YouTube channel.

Postings included links to extremist sites and messages discouraging students from attending school events that did not 'adhere to a particular religious viewpoint'. One warned that any student who attended a leavers' party or indulged in 'free mixing' and 'listening to music' would face severe consequences later, the report reveals.

The report shows that the school's senior leadership team and governors had reacted inadequately to warnings given earlier this year by counter-terrorism police. Arrangements for vetting visiting speakers and monitoring student groups were 'not robust enough'.

Communication between the head, Haydn Evans, members of the senior leadership team, and governors was poor, inspectors found.

A statement from the London Diocesan Board for Schools (LDBS) said that urgent action was already under way to tackle the issues raised by OFSTED. 'Extremism has no place in our society, especially not in our schools.' Diocesan staff are understood to be involved in an improvement plan, which draws on the anti-radicalisation Prevent programme, now in place at Sir John Cass. They hope that the school, which will be subject to frequent visits from OFSTED inspectors, could regain its former Outstanding rating by Easter.

Mr Evans briefed parents about the OFSTED report, and the measures being taken in response, at special meetings last Friday. They were chaired by the Revd Trevor Critchlow, Rector of St Dunstan's, Stepney, and the new chairman at Sir John Cass, and attracted a high turnout, it was reported.

Sir John Cass and Redcoat is the only C of E school so far to be inspected in relation to the Government's anti-extremism agenda. The criticisms it faces are vastly different from those levelled at the Birmingham schools – none of them faith schools – involved in the 'Trojan Horse' inquiry (News, 24 October).

Where inspectors in Birmingham found evidence of co-ordinated efforts by some teachers and governors to make their schools more compliant with a conservative form of Islam, Sir John Cass senior teachers and governors are criticised for failing to monitor the internet activity and behaviour of some of their sixth-formers.

The Chief Inspector, Sir Michael Wilshaw, also appears to draw a sharp distinction, in his advice note to the Secretary of State, Nicky Morgan, between the findings of the snap inspection of Sir John Cass and OFSTED's simultaneous unannounced visits to six independent Muslim schools, two of them connected to the East London Mosque.

All six were found to be inadequate in all respects, the general curriculum compromised by concentration on Islamic teaching. Sir Michael recommends that the Education Secretary use powers under the Education Act 2002, likely to lead to closure.

In the case of Sir John Cass, he promises robust evaluation of school and local-authority improvement plans, and early special-measures monitoring visits.

As news of the downgrading of Sir John Cass was made public, parents, former pupils and other locals piled in with praise for the much loved school, which is a beacon of success in a deeply disadvantaged area. Heads of neighbouring schools rushed to the defence of the head of Sir John Cass. Mr Evans was appointed CBE in the last New Year Honours list for his stewardship of the school for nearly 20 years. Earlier this month, he was awarded an honorary degree by the University of East London for the same reason.

Sir John Cass and Redcoat was a failing school when Mr Evans took over in 1995. He introduced rules that improved standards of behaviour and academic achievement. By 2004, the school was seen by OFSTED as a model for educating pupils of Bangladeshi and similar backgrounds. In 2008, it was rated Outstanding.

Mr Evans was reportedly 'shell-shocked' by the result of the snap inspection. A response from Tower Hamlets Council emphasising the overall success of the school included a brief statement from Mr Evans. He was 'surprised' by the finding. His priority was to rectify the problems OFSTED had identified, the statement said.

28 November 2014

⇨ The above information is reprinted with kind permisison from *Church Times*. Please visit www.churchtimes.co.uk.

What makes a school susceptible to radicalisation? Here is what Ofsted found

Ofsted's findings at seven schools – one state and six independent – inspected in Tower Hamlets, east London has caused another outcry across the country. But what exactly did they find in these schools that seemed to suggest that pupils might be susceptible to radicalisation. And are the findings really such a cause for concern?

Sir John Cass Foundation and Redcoat Church of England Secondary School

This secondary state school, which includes a sixth form, was the only state school included in the series of Ofsted inspections.

The watchdog declared the school – which had previously been rated as outstanding – as inadequate, due to concerns about the sixth form, leadership and management and the behaviour and safety of pupils.

Inspectors warned that the school had failed to respond properly to concerns raised by police in 2013/14 about social media websites bearing the name of a school sixth-form society which had links to individuals associated with extremism. Senior staff and governors had failed to inform students or parents of this serious concern.

The report concluded that the sixth form was inadequate 'because students have not been given sufficient guidance on the dangers associated with using the Internet, particularly in relation to extremist views.'

It also said that the school's checks for vetting visiting speakers and monitoring the activities of student groups were not good enough to ensure that pupils were kept safe and found that neither staff nor governors had been given training in how to identify and respond to early signs of extremism or radicalisation.

Ofsted's inspection report revealed that leaders had organised separate boys' and girls' entrances and exits, and there were segregated outdoor and indoor spaces at break time and lunchtime.

'As a consequence, boys and girls do not have equal access to the school's facilities. For example, girls cannot use the football cages provided in the boys' playground. In the sixth form, girls say that they do not go into the mixed common room, resulting in boys and girls segregating into two separate areas.

'Little understanding is shown by students or staff as to the reasons for this separation. The consequence is the limiting of opportunities for boys and girls to interact socially and develop skills for life in modern Britain.'

The report did rate the school 'good' for quality of teaching and achievement of pupils.

Tony Mullee, chief executive of Sir John Cass's Foundation, said the Foundation is 'greatly concerned' by the Ofsted report and is committed to addressing the issues raised and in the coming weeks will be assessing the action needed to return the school to 'outstanding'.

Mazahirul Uloom School

Inspectors found that the curriculum at this private Islamic boys' secondary school was too narrow, often focusing only on Muslim faith and culture. Pupils had 'very few' chances to meet those from other backgrounds and as a result did not have a decent understanding of different faiths and cultures.

'Several students told an inspector that it would be wrong to learn about other religions,' the report found, adding 'students are not being prepared for life in a diverse British society.'

The report went on to say that pupils were given no lessons in drama, music or art, while opportunities for creativity in other subjects were 'too limited'.

'The curriculum does not promote students' understanding of the fundamental British rule of law. When discussing sharia law and English law, they were unable to tell inspectors which laws they should follow, and which were more important.

'The school does not actively promote principles that encourage students to have respect for those with different backgrounds. For example, students presented a narrow view of the role of females in society. Some students told inspectors that "women stay at home and clean and look after the children. They cook and pray and wait for us to come back in from school and help with homework".'

Inspectors warned that the school had failed to carry out decent background checks on staff who had lived or worked overseas, failed to take up references from previous employers

and not checked whether teachers were banned from the profession.

They also found a locked staff bedroom on a corridor next to classrooms, with the principal unable to say who slept in the room, and raised concerns about health and safety after finding an unlocked kitchen with a sharp knife left on a worktop and insecure entrances to the school from the front entrance and through the mosque.

The school premises were also found to be in a poor condition, with a poorly kept and unclean washing area in the basement, with cracked and missing tiles, unclean grouting and an unhygienic, dirty bin.

The snap inspection was conducted at the request of the Department for Education (DfE) and overall, inspectors identified areas were independent school standards were unmet.

London East Academy

The school is a selective Islamic secondary school for boys with 150 students. Inspectors judged the leadership, behaviour and safety of pupils, the achievement of pupils and the quality of teaching as 'inadequate'.

The report said students' development was 'restricted by their lack of experiences in creative and aesthetic subjects' and there were 'insufficient' resources to teach humanities subjects adequately.

It did find that the school's executive headteacher has implemented a number of initiatives to 'remind students of their responsibilities as British citizens' and teachers were 'keen for students to widen their horizons and become active members of British society'.

Pupils were taught to obey the laws of British society but, Ofsted said, their 'spiritual, moral, social and cultural development is weak' and they have 'insufficient understanding of how other people live, both in Britain and abroad'.

Inspectors were aware that 'serious allegations of a child protection nature were being investigated by the appropriate authorities,' the report said. It described the school's safeguarding of students as 'inadequate', adding: 'Parts of

the building are open to members of the public, allowing them to have unauthorised access to students and staff.'

Al-Mizan School

This selective independent Islamic school for boys aged between seven and 11 was also found to be 'inadequate' in the four key areas.

Inspectors found the range of subjects taught was too narrow and said the school 'does not promote pupils' understanding of different cultures and religions', adding: 'The school does not prepare pupils for life in modern Britain.'

It said that although the school's website says pupils are taught the National Curriculum, 'in practice, this does not happen'. Pupils told inspectors they are not taught music, while some of their books for humanities subjects showed only one piece of work since September.

The report added that work in religious studies books shows that many pupils have only learnt about Islam.

Work is not marked adequately, with mistakes in spelling, punctuation and grammar often left uncorrected, Ofsted said. A fifth of pupils do not attend school regularly, the report said.

Some classrooms were found to be 'disorganised and untidy' with 'pupils surrounded by piles of unwanted books and paper'.

Both London East Academy and Al-Mizan School are based in the London Muslim Centre.

In a joint statement the two schools said they are 'already working hard to address weaknesses identified in Ofsted's recent reports', insisting that both have 'enjoyed an excellent reputation to date'.

Ebrahim Academy

This Muslim independent secondary school in Tower Hamlets has been flagged as 'inadequate' after inspectors warned that it was failing to prepare students for life in modern Britain and to properly promote British values.

The Ofsted report criticised the school for failing to ensure that staff

do not promote 'partisan political values' or that when such issues are discussed, opposing views are also presented, and for its narrow curriculum, which excludes creative skills and appreciation for the arts.

'The curriculum is too narrow,' the watchdog found. 'It does not prepare students for life in modern Britain. There is no provision for developing students' creative skills or aesthetic appreciation.'

It also found that staff had not been given training on identifying extremist views, and were unaware of the local council's anti-radicalism strategy, Prevent.

In one case, it said: 'One member of staff stated he had identified extremist views in a student's writing but he did not share these concerns with leaders.'

While the governing body was aware of the school's shortcomings it had failed to act to improve standards, the report said.

It concluded: 'Leaders have created a climate where students develop a positive attitude to their own faith and to learning.

'However, the school does not actively and systematically promote fundamental British values.'

The report did note that students were keen to do well and are polite.

'They are tolerant and respectful of people of other faiths and cultures'.

Jamiatul Ummah School

Inspectors found that the curriculum at this boys' selective independent school was too narrow, with too few opportunities to promote personal, social and health education, citizenship or careers.

There was a good range of opportunities for students to study and practise their Islamic faith, the report said.

But it added: 'In other respects students are not provided with a broad and balanced curriculum. Students do not have opportunities to learn about music or art. Design and technology education is not provided.

'There are very few opportunities to develop students' creativity in physical education, such as through gymnastics or dance. The narrowness of the curriculum means that students' spiritual, moral, social and cultural education, in particular their understanding of the fundamental British values of democracy, the rule of law, individual liberty and mutual respect and tolerance, is underdeveloped.

'Not enough time is allocated for personal, social and health education, or to raise their understanding of citizenship and careers.'

Ofsted warned that the school was failing to comply with legal requirements for making checks on staff, putting students' safety at risk.

And it said that the school's building was 'shabby and dirty and in need of significant repair'.

'The flooring in corridors and staircases is badly worn. One staircase does not have a bannister. Some stairwells contain old furniture and rubbish. Boxes of books stored on the floor in the library present a hazard. Students have to get changed for PE lessons publicly in the dining hall. Only one shower is provided nearby for use by all students. There are no washing facilities in the first aid room.'

Despite these concerns, inspectors did find that students say they feel safe in the school and bullying is rare.

It added that pupils' behaviour is good, and that youngsters were pleasant and polite.

In response to the findings, the school said it was 'profoundly disappointed' by the report, adding it is committed to achieving excellence and continuous improvement.

It said it accepts the conclusions and will be working to make the required improvements.

But the school added it believes Ofsted has given 'disproportionate emphasis to certain issues which do not reflect the real characteristics of the school and has not portrayed accurately the school or given appropriate weight to the varied educational experiences, including national curriculum.'

21 November 2014

⇨ The above information is reprinted with kind permission from Asian Image. Please visit www.asianimage.co.uk for further information.

Families who fear ISIS is targeting their children urged to lock up their passports

Islamist extremists use grooming methods of paedophiles, says counter-terror group.

By Tracy McVeigh and Tess Reidy

Parents have been urged to keep their children's passports under 'lock and key' if they feel they are at risk of being groomed online by Islamist extremists.

As the Prime Minister expressed deep concern over the disappearance of the three east London schoolgirls who are thought to be on their way to join Islamic State (ISIS) fighters in Syria, the head of Inspire, a human rights organisation working with Muslim women, called on schools to do more to burst the 'romanticised notion' of ISIS that is being peddled to young people by a slick online propaganda machine.

The head of Inspire, Sara Khan, said the tactics used by those luring young girls to Syria and Iraq to marry them off to jihadis or force them into domestic servitude, were the grooming methods of paedophiles.

'We need to stop using the phrase "jihadi brides",' she said. 'This is grooming, a child safety issue, and we need to make that distinction. These are normal teenage girls who should be in school, with their families, and have sacrificed everything to run off and join this crazed group.

'Everyone has a role to play now. Schools need support so they can start talking about this, they mustn't shy away from discussing these topics. They need to be saying to girls: "Do you understand the realities of Isis? Do you understand what life would be like?"'

Khan added: 'They are getting all their info online where it's so glorified and romantic. Like it's all one big happy family out there. Well it isn't. Parents need help and the most practical suggestion I can make is keep your daughter's passport under lock and key.' Inspire launches a campaign on Monday called Making a Stand, to help parents cope with the ISIS threat.

The three missing girls, Shamima Begum, 15, Kadiza Sultana, 16, and 15-year-old Amira Abase, all attend Bethnal Green Academy where they are said to be top students.

They left the UK unchallenged on a lunchtime flight to Istanbul on Tuesday and security camera images of them at Gatwick airport were released on Thursday by police. Commander Richard Walton said there was still a chance the girls could be found and stopped from crossing into Syria, especially as snowstorms were affecting transport out of Istanbul.

Police confirmed that the three had been spoken to by officers who were making inquiries over their friend, a 15-year-old from the same school, who ran away to Syria in December. 'There was nothing to suggest at the time that the girls themselves were at risk and indeed their disappearance has come as a great surprise, not least to their own families,' said Walton.

A 17-year-old from Hackney who said she was a friend of Shamima and her sister told the *Observer* that the teenager loved music and film. 'I can't believe she's done this.

'It's a change in Shamima that has come about very quickly. But I could see that on her Twitter she had some dodgy religious people that you don't want to know.'

David Cameron also called for schools to take a role. 'The fight against Islamic extremism is not just one that we can wage by the police and border control.

'It needs every school, every university, every college, every community to recognise that they have a role to play.'

At the East London Mosque, worshippers were shocked at the girls' disappearance. Bil Hassan, 27, from Tower Hamlets, said: 'You look at the pictures and they look like lovely girls. That's the shocking element of it. These aren't scary faces, theses are young girls. There are a lot of theories of why they went – grooming, love for ISIS – but people are driven by a sense of adventure and that is part of it.'

Dr Zaza Elsheikh said: 'They want a sense of belonging and seek excitement in the same way that people join gangs. They believe going to Syria is better than their lives here. They are small fish and they want something bigger.

'Parents aren't able to connect with their social media and check up on them. These men out there want someone to cook and clean. They are being fed a big fat lie. This is grooming.'

21 February 2015

⇨ The above information is reprinted with kind permission from *The Guardian*. Please visit www.theguardian.com for further information.

Violence in Britain: how the war on terror criminalises ordinary people

THE CONVERSATION

An article from The Conversation.

By Vicki Sentas, Lecturer in Law at UNSW Australia

It is now accepted that the war on terror has generated an extensive repertoire of its very own terror. Drone strikes resulting in extrajudicial killings, rendition and torture – zones of exception like Guantanamo Bay come to mind, as does Britain's complicity in extraordinary rendition and torture.

Then there are the normalised, everyday forms of terror operational in Britain that rarely register as state-sanctioned violence because they are understood to keep us safe. This includes MI5 and police raids without charge, compulsory schedule 7 detention and questioning and stop and search of communities made suspect.

Even less visible as state violence is the global regime of targeted sanctions against non-state armed actors and those even indirectly connected to them. UN Security Council Resolution 1373 requires states to establish their own domestic banning regimes in order to criminalise the support and financing for terrorism. Variously referred to as 'blacklisting', 'banning' or 'proscription', the designation of organisations and individuals as terrorist has been under scrutiny for bearing all the hallmarks of authoritarian dictatorships.

These forms of 'lawfare', including the Terrorism Act 2000 (UK), criminalise diverse forms of association and support, without requiring intentional acts of violence against civilians. This creates serious consequences for many diaspora in the UK – including Tamils, Kurds, Baluch and Palestinians – who remain connected to armed struggles for self-determination by virtue of being a people with a shared historical and political culture.

Terrorist listing makes no distinction between armed conflicts and terrorism. Worse, listing transforms diverse armed conflicts into terrorism in spite of whether armed groups are fighting an authoritarian regime or responding to state terror. Clearly, many non-state armed groups have terrorised and killed civilians and breached the laws of war. But by labelling non-state actors as *a priori* terrorists, the political claims of non-state actors, and the root causes of armed conflicts, are denied and diverse forms of state terror are legitimated as 'counter-terrorism'.

This effect has been described by international legal jurist Antonio Cassese as institutionalised violence. Banning organisations is a tool of British foreign policy which functions as institutionalised state violence in three key ways: firstly by denying the application of international law and principles of self-determination; secondly, by foreclosing opportunities for peaceful settlement of conflict; and thirdly, by legitimating and facilitating state terror and repressions and in some cases the war crimes of other states.

Turning armed conflict into terrorism

The UK has been proscribing organisations since listing Northern Irish groups, most notably through the Prevention of Terrorism Act 1974. More than 60 militant non-state actors are currently banned in the UK (as of April 2014). Some of these actors have used armed conflict to further political claims for statehood, regional autonomy or ethno-cultural rights and have a broad support base – for example, the Baluch, Palestinians, Tamils, Basque, among other peoples.

Some non-state armed groups (and nation states) breach the laws of war by targeting civilians. But listing does nothing to stop the use of terror by either side. The idea is that by criminalising the broadest range of relationships connected to armed conflict, Britain can de-legitimise the organisation and eradicate its support base. What does this look like when the support base for an armed conflict demands recognition of minority cultures and languages, accountability for state crimes and an end to conflict? Let's take the example of how the Kurdish struggle for self-determination in Turkey has been transformed into 'terrorism'.

The Kurdistan Workers' Party (PKK) is listed by Britain as a terrorist organisation, yet the PKK is currently engaged in fragile negotiations for peace with Turkey. Meanwhile, listing of the PKK as terrorist by the international community has given Turkey the confidence and legitimacy to

embark on a mass criminalisation of Kurdish civil society. Between 2009 and the start of 2013, almost 40,000 people were prosecuted for 'membership of a terrorist organisation' in Turkey, according to government statistics.

In its campaign to urge the British Government to lift its ban against the PKK, the campaign group Peace in Kurdistan argues that the ban 'distorts the whole political process by ensuring that anyone who expresses an opinion on controversial issues in Turkey can be held to be an associate of terrorism and prosecuted with the full force of a law that is as indiscriminate as it is unjust'.

In Britain, Kurds are routinely criminalised and terrorised by the fact of this proscription, but no-one has been convicted of any offences. This is because the Home Office identifies 'disruption' of forms of association and material support, rather than prosecution, as the key object of the proscription regime. The UK positions itself 'at the forefront of EU member states' action against the PKK'. Kurdish activists are routinely harassed by police and intelligence agencies in the UK, often as part of co-ordinated operations targeting Kurds across Europe.

For example, in 2011, more than a dozen Kurds were sent

the message by MI5 that their fundraising for charities, campaign work and their organising in community centres should stop, or they would face deportation or criminal charges. On 10 January 2013, Kurdish families travelling to Paris were detained for seven hours at a Dover crossing, under the notorious schedule 7 of the Terrorism Act 2000, which allows for detention and questioning on suspicion of terrorism without reasonable cause or access to the usual legal rights. The families were travelling to attend a demonstration to commemorate the assassination of three Kurdish activists in which the Turkish state is allegedly implicated. The significant effects of routine, everyday forms of arbitrary state interference are to disrupt collective, political life.

Proscription laws seek to disrupt the collective organisation of Kurdish people because they are understood to 'legitimate' the PKK's political claims and, therefore, they can only be understood as supporting violence. More broadly, the proscription regime as it is constituted globally means that G8 states claiming democratic credentials create the conditions for state terror by less powerful nations. Proscription creates an international regime in which some states are empowered to use more repressive tactics against movements for self-determination. The British state, among other states who ban armed conflicts, deserves sustained attention for its role in depoliticising self-determination movements and legitimising and therefore extending state violence elsewhere.

13 May 2014

⇨ The above information is reprinted with kind permission from The Conversation. Please visit www.theconversation. com for further information.

Battle against ISIS: plan to charge jihadists with treason 'will not work', claims terror expert

Moves to prosecute Britons returning from Iraq and Syria would be counter-productive, Professor Peter Neumann to tell MPs.

By Jonathan Owen

Britain's 'lock-them-up' approach to dealing with returning British jihadist fighters is doomed to failure and risks making it harder to find potential terrorists, warned one of the world's leading terror experts yesterday.

'Britain needs a more differentiated strategy towards people returning from conflict in Syria and Iraq,' said Professor Peter Neumann, director of the International Centre for the Study of Radicalisation at King's College London.

Professor Neumann will tell MPs in Parliament tomorrow that a punitive approach, which includes prosecuting people for treason, is misguided. 'Right now the strategy is very much we're going to lock them up – we're going to try them for treason. It's a strategy that is based basically only on a punitive approach.' The academic, a senior adviser on the UN Security Council resolution introduced by President Obama earlier this year, calling for global action to tackle the threat, added: 'While that may be correct for some, there are also a number of other categories of people that could be dealt with differently.'

His criticism of the Government's anti-terror response follows that of former Director of Public Prosecutions, Lord Macdonald QC, who said charging returning jihadists with treason was 'a juvenile response to a grown-up problem'.

It comes after claims to MPs last week by the Foreign Secretary, Philip Hammond, that Britons who fight for Islamic State (ISIS) or swear allegiance to the group could be charged with treason. The Foreign Secretary admitted there were talks within the Government about resurrecting the law, which can carry a life sentence. It is the latest in a series of draconian measures being considered by the Government, which also include anti-social behaviour orders for extremists and tougher laws to make it illegal to join extremist groups, even those not directly involved in terrorism.

Professor Neumann said that people returning from Syria broadly fell into one of three categories: the dangerous, the disturbed and the disillusioned. Those deemed a danger should be imprisoned, but some will be traumatised by their experiences and 'need psychological help more than prison'. Others will be 'disillusioned people who have become disenchanted with IS, who never really joined in the first place and who just want to reintegrate into British society, and these people should be supported because they could become very powerful voices speaking out against Isis'.

Hundreds of veterans from Syria are already back in Britain. 'So it's not a future problem – it's a problem that already exists,' he said. 'The Government does not know the identities and whereabouts of every single one of those 250 people. If you have only the punitive approach then these people will not come forward.'

There are now thousands of foreign fighters in Syria, including hundreds of Britons. About 30 British jihadists are believed to have died fighting alongside ISIS and other groups in Syria. Britain's most senior counter-terrorism police officer, Assistant Commissioner Mark Rowley, warned last week that operations against Syria-linked threats are at an 'exceptionally high' level, with

more than 200 anti-terrorism arrests across Britain this year. Although at least 500 jihadists are suspected of travelling abroad, only 16 returning from Syria have been charged under the Terrorism Act, which outlaws training and preparing for terrorist acts. Three have been convicted.

Government officials know they cannot convict everyone, claimed Professor Neumann. 'The reality is that, as people in the Home Office have told me, there is not necessarily enough evidence for everyone to be convicted.' This risks a significant number being acquitted and 'beyond the control of the security forces altogether'. Jailing jihadists carries its own risk – 'putting a large number of potentially highly radicalised people into a system where they can spread their ideology further'.

The rise of women within the ranks of jihadists has taken experts by surprise, he admitted. 'Ten to 15 years ago, if you were looking at home-grown extremism in the UK, it would be very rare to see females involved. Now, in most European countries we have between ten and 15 per cent women, often without prior association in the extremist movement, who have gone to Syria to support Isis.' They are not there as fighters but 'on the ground in supportive functions', he added. Women should be viewed as 'potential recruits' but are being 'largely ignored by current government approaches' which view them 'typically as some positive influence on the men within their family'. This is one of the reasons why Professor Neumann and others have been calling for the Prevent counter-terror strategy to be 'completely recalibrated'.

The terror expert accused the Government of failing to match its words with actions. 'The Government says this is the greatest extremist threat that Britain has faced for a generation, yet at the same time, at the policy level we haven't seen the amount or the degree of engagement that would be necessary if it really was the biggest threat, so there's a disconnect here,' he said. 'They need to match the rhetoric with actual policy action on the ground.'

19 October 2014

⇨ The above information is reprinted with kind permission from *The Independent*. Please visit www.independent.co.uk for further information.

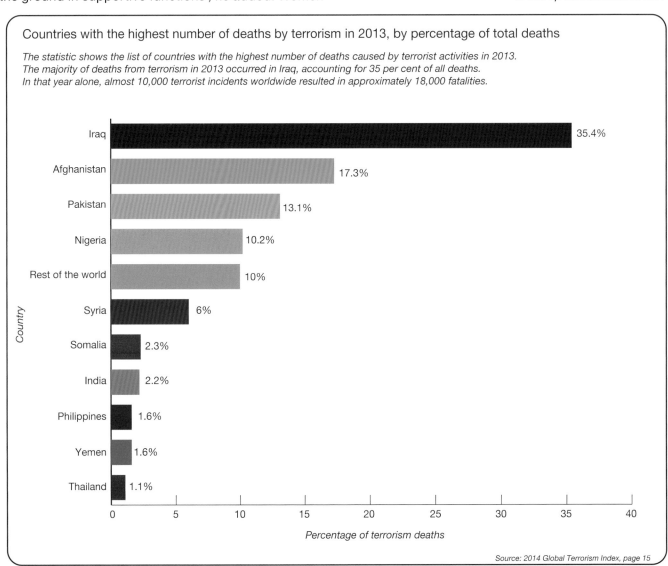

Countries with the highest number of deaths by terrorism in 2013, by percentage of total deaths

The statistic shows the list of countries with the highest number of deaths caused by terrorist activities in 2013.
The majority of deaths from terrorism in 2013 occurred in Iraq, accounting for 35 per cent of all deaths.
In that year alone, almost 10,000 terrorist incidents worldwide resulted in approximately 18,000 fatalities.

Country	Percentage of terrorism deaths
Iraq	35.4%
Afghanistan	17.3%
Pakistan	13.1%
Nigeria	10.2%
Rest of the world	10%
Syria	6%
Somalia	2.3%
India	2.2%
Philippines	1.6%
Yemen	1.6%
Thailand	1.1%

Source: 2014 Global Terrorism Index, page 15

Are you worried about someone you know who could be involved in terrorism or violent extremism?

It can be hard to think that someone you know or are close to could be involved in something that may hurt or kill people. But there's plenty you can do to help them and help entire communities.

What can you do?

It can be incredibly dangerous getting mixed up in violent extremist activity. If you think they will listen, talk to them, try to persuade them that they should think about what they're doing or encourage them to talk to someone such as:

⇨ their parents, teacher or other responsible adult

⇨ a professional at ChildLine who can offer help and advice in confidence.

If you don't think they'll listen to you, talk to someone yourself - such as your own parents or other family member.

Every local community in London has a Local Policing Team which is a team of local police officers who can help to deal with local problems. They can be contacted on 101 or through www. met.police.uk.

Remember – it's far better if the person you're worried about gets help now before they do anything that could lead to people being hurt.

Some important things to think about terrorism

Yes, we all need to take this seriously, but you shouldn't let the fear of it alter your daily life.

Don't let the threat of terrorism stop you travelling on the tube or bus, or going out and doing the things you normally do.

⇨ The above information is reprinted with kind permission from the Metropolitan Police Service. Please visit safe.met.police.uk for further information.

© Metropolitan Police Service 2015

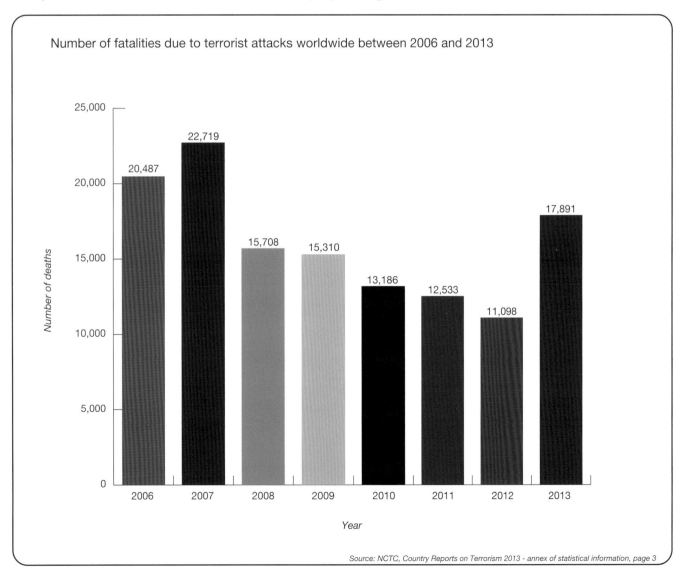

Number of fatalities due to terrorist attacks worldwide between 2006 and 2013

Number of deaths

Year	Deaths
2006	20,487
2007	22,719
2008	15,708
2009	15,310
2010	13,186
2011	12,533
2012	11,098
2013	17,891

Year

Source: NCTC, Country Reports on Terrorism 2013 - annex of statistical information, page 3

Key facts

- In Pakistan, between 2004 and 2013, there were 724 attacks against educational institutions, compared to 213 in Thailand and 205 in Afghanistan

- Al-Qaeda in Iraq were responsible for 492 terrorist attacks between 2000 and 2013. (page 4)

- Boko Haram were responsible for 750 terrorist attacks between 2000 and 2013. (page 4)

- Over the last 12 months, global fatalities from acts of terrorism have risen 30% compared to the previous five-year average. (page 5)

- Globally, the Maplecroft Terrorism and Security Dashboard (MTSD) recorded 18,668 fatalities in the 12 months prior to 1 July, up 29.3% from an annual average of 14,433 for the previous five years. (page 5)

- The MTSD classifies 12 countries as 'extreme risk', many of which are blighted by high levels of instability and weak governance. (page 5)

- Iraq, rated as the highest risk country in the MTSD, recorded more than three times as many acts of terrorism as Pakistan (which had the second highest number of incidents) – with 3,158 acts of terrorism, resulting in 5,929 fatalities. (page 6)

- Nigeria has been host to 146 reported attacks in the period 1 July 2013 to 30 June 2014, resulting in 3,477 killed – an average of 24 people killed per attack, compared to two deaths per attack in Iraq. (page 6)

- 72% of terrorist attacks between 1970 and 2012 occurred during a period of major conflict. (page 6)

- The UK terror threat level was only made public for the first time in the wake of the 7 July attacks in London in 2005. (page 7)

- The UK terror threat level stood at severe for 18 months [between January 2010 and July 2011] before being lowered to substantial for three years. (page 7)

- The authors of the official report into the killing [of an off-duty solider named Lee Rigby] chastised Facebook for not picking up on the threat, arguing there was a 'significant possibility' that the attack could have been prevented if the technology company had alerted the authorities. (page 8)

- Michael Stephens, Deputy Director, Qatar, for the Royal United Services Institute (RUSI), says there could be as many as 300 Britons fighting for ISIS, and a further almost 300 other Europeans. (page 10)

- In 2013, there were a total of 2,990 kidnappings due to terrorism worldwide. (page 13)

- This year's report, by the Institute for Economics and Peace, recorded nearly 10,000 terrorist attacks and 18,000 deaths in 2013, a 60 per cent rise from the previous year. The vast majority of attacks – 66 per cent – were perpetrated by just four groups: ISIS (Islamic State), Boko Haram, the Taliban and Al-Qaeda. All of these groups follow a Wahhabi ideology. More than 80 per cent of deaths from terrorism in 2013 occurred in just five countries – Iraq, Afghanistan, Pakistan, Nigeria and Syria. (page 16)

- In a new raft of Saudi Arabian laws, atheists are being defined as terrorists. (page 17)

- 11% of people questioned, strongly agree with the statement, 'Differences in culture and values make future conflict between British born Muslims and white Britons inevitable.' (page 19)

- The maximum period of detention without charge for most criminal suspects is 24 to 96 hours. But, between 2006 and 2011, terrorism suspects could be detained for up to 28 days without charge. (page 26)

- After the tragic events of 11 September 2001, emergency laws were passed which allowed for the indefinite detention of foreign nationals, who were suspected of being terrorists. Under this law, individuals could be detained for an unlimited period at a maximum security prison despite never being charged, let alone convicted, of any offence. (page 27)

- Security service estimates suggest around 500 Britons have travelled to Syria to take part in the civil war. (page 28)

- Although at least 500 jihadists are suspected of travelling abroad, only 16 returning from Syria have been charged under the Terrorism Act, which outlaws training and preparing for terrorist acts. Three have been convicted. (page 37)

Al-Qaeda

A group/organisation of Islamic militants, responsible for the 9/11 attacks in America.

Atheism

Atheism refers to the firm belief that there is no god or divine power at work in the universe, and human beings are constrained to one life only, with no continued existence after death.

Counter-terrorism

Counter-terrorism refers to the tactics and techniques used by governments and other groups to prevent or minimise a terrorist threat.

Extraordinary rendition

Rendition is the arrest and transference of a fugitive from one country or state to another and is an acceptable legal practice. When it takes place without the approval of a judicial authority, however, or where the suspect is afterwards tortured in breach of their human rights, it is known as `extraordinary rendition`. The USA has been accused of this practice with the alleged complicity of other Western nations, including the UK.

Extremism

Extremism refers to beliefs or practices that are seen as radical, and can give rise to militance. Groups justifying their violence on Islamic grounds, such as Al-Qaeda

ISIS

ISIS stands for 'the Islamic State of Iraq and al-Sham'. It is an extreme jihadi group that now controls a large territory in western Iraq and eastern Syria.

Islam

Islam is the second largest faith group in the UK today - 2.8% of the UK population were Muslims in 2001, according to the last census. Muslims believe in the word of Allah (God) as set out in their holy book, the Qur`an, by the prophet Muhammed in Arabia 1,300 years ago. Islam is a way of life, and followers must observe strict rules regarding diet, lifestyle and worship.

The Human Rights Act

The Human Rights Act is a written law (statute) passed in 1998 which is in force in England and Wales. The rights that are protected by this law are based on the articles of the European Convention on Human Rights. There is an ongoing debate between supporters of the Act and its critics as to whether it should be kept, or replaced with a new UK Bill of Rights.

Radicalisation

The process by which a person, or group of people, adopt extreme religious, political or ideological beliefs.

September eleventh (9/11)

9/11 is a common way of referring to the events of 11 September 2001, the date on which four passenger planes were hijacked by Al-Qaeda militants and flown into US targets - notably the twin towers of the World Trade Center in New York - causing thousands of lives to be lost. These attacks were significant in bringing terrorism into the international spotlight, changing the world`s political climate and launching the `War on Terror`.

Terrorism

The word `terrorism` dates back to the 18th century, but there is no globally accepted definition of the term. The most widely accepted is probably that put forward by the US State Department, which states that terrorism is `premeditated, politically motivated violence perpetrated against non-combatant targets by subnational groups or clandestine agents, usually intended to influence an audience.` Types include Nationalist-Separatist, Religious, Right-Wing and Left-Wing Terrorism.

The 7/7 bombings

Also know as the London bombings, this refers to the events of 7 July 2005, when four suicide bombers took the lives of 56 people on the London transport system. The incident was the deadliest single act of terrorism in the UK since Lockerbie (the 1988 bombing of Pan Am Flight 103 which killed 270), and the deadliest bombing in London since the Second World War. The attacks were significant in drawing UK attention to the terrorism problem - they demonstrated that terrorism could occur at home as well as abroad, and could even be perpetrated by British citizens (three of the four bombers were British).

The Taliban

A militant Islamist group which ruled large parts of Afghanistan between 1996 and 2001.

Treason

The crime of betraying one's country.

Violent extremism

When violence is used to achieve or promote radical/ extreme religious, political or ideological beliefs.

Assignments

Brainstorming

⇨ In small groups, discuss what you know about terrorism and extremism. Consider the following?

- What is terrorism?
- What is extremism?
- What is the difference between terrorism and extremism?
- What are some of the reasons people commit acts of terrorism or violent extremism?

Research

⇨ Do some research about terrorist attacks in the UK. Choose an event from the last 20 years and write some notes about what happened, the cause and the effects. Share with your class.

⇨ Choose one of the countries highlighted in red on the Terrorism and Security Dashboard, on page six, and use newspaper archives to find out about recent terrorist activity in that country. Write some notes and share with a partner.

⇨ Research anti-terror laws in the UK and then compare them to anti-terror laws in the US. Write some notes on your findings.

⇨ In pairs, research the current terror threat level in the UK. You should find out:

- Which groups are most strongly linked to terrorist activity in the UK and aboard?
- What are these groups trying to achieve?
- What is being done to combat these threats?

Design

⇨ Design a poster that could be displayed in public places to demonstrate what members of the public should do if they suspect someone they know is involved in terrorism or violent extremism.

⇨ Choose one of the articles in this book and create an illustration to highlight the key themes/message of your chosen article.

⇨ Using the table on page four, create a graph or infographic to create a visual representation of the data.

⇨ There is increasing concern for young people who are being drawn into violent extremism. Create a leaflet that gives help and advice to family members who are worried that a son/daughter, friend or relative is affected.

Oral

⇨ 'Social media platforms like Twitter and Facebook are dangerous and encourage people to become terrorists or extremists.' Debate this statement in small groups, then write down your main thoughts/comments and share with the rest of your class.

⇨ 'One man's terrorist is another man's freedom fighter.' Discuss your views on the meaning behind this phrase and summarise your thoughts in the form of an essay, referring to at least two historical or current figures in your answer: for example, Malcolm X, Nelson Mandela, Martin McGuinness.

⇨ Choose one of the illustrations in this book and, in pairs, discuss what you think the artist was trying to portray with their image.

⇨ Mohammed Emwazi, also known as, Jihadi John has received a lot of media attention. Do you think this kind of publicity encourages terrorism and extremism? Discuss as a class.

⇨ 'Primary school children are too young to learn about terrorism.' Discuss this statement with a partner.

Reading/writing

⇨ Write a one-paragraph definition of violent extremism.

⇨ 'Religious extremism is now the main driving force of terrorism worldwide.' Write an essay exploring this statement. You should write at least two sides of A4.

⇨ Read *The Reluctant Fundamentalist* by Mohsin Hamid, or watch the film of the same name, write a review exploring the theme of fundamentalism in the novel/film.

⇨ Write an article exploring the human rights issues surrounding anti-terrorism laws in the UK. You should write no more than two-sides of A4.

⇨ Read the article *Universities must not become part of the security apparatus* on page 29. Do you agree or disagree with the author? Write a blog post exploring your opinion.

⇨ Do you think schools have a responsibility to teach pupils about terrorism and extremism? Will the recent emphasis on 'fundamental British values' help to prevent radicalisation? Write a letter to your head teacher exploring your feelings about these questions.

⇨ Research the 2014 Trojan Horse scandal surrounding extremism in Birmingham schools. Write an article, suitable for your local or school newspaper, outlining your findings.

Acknowledgements

The publisher is grateful for permission to reproduce the material in this book. While every care has been taken to trace and acknowledge copyright, the publisher tenders its apology for any accidental infringement or where copyright has proved untraceable. The publisher would be pleased to come to a suitable arrangement in any such case with the rightful owner.

Images
All images courtesy of iStock, except page 12 © watchsmart (Flickr) and page 37 © Morguefile.

Illustrations
Don Hatcher: pages 1 & 19. Simon Kneebone: pages 15 & 32. Angelo Madrid: pages 8 & 22.

Additional acknowledgements

Editorial on behalf of Independence Educational Publishers by Cara Acred.

With thanks to the Independence team: Mary Chapman, Sandra Dennis, Christina Hughes, Jackie Staines and Jan Sunderland.

Cara Acred

Cambridge

May 2015